Stilettos on Gridiron

Women Getting a Feel for the Game

with Former NFL Player Reginald "Reggie" Jones

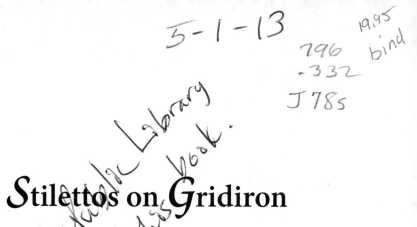

Published by Fit-2-Win/RJ Speaks, 2013

Stilettos on Gridiron: Women Getting a Feel for the Game with Former NFL Player Reginald "Reggie" Jones

Written by Reginald "Reggie" Jones

ISBN: 978-0-9888804-0-5

First published in the United States of America, 2013
Publisher: Fit-2-Win/RJ Speaks
website: www.fit-2-win.com

For information, or to book Reginald to speak for your company, organization or university, email Reginald Jones: rjwrites@fit-2-win.com

Cover photo/design: Ray White Photography

Acknowledgements

*F*irst, to my wife, Cynthia, and daughter, Kristin, thank you both for enduring the many long hours and isolation over the last year as I worked to see this project through. Now you'll get to enjoy the ride. Well, for a while—because the next book project will be starting soon.

In addition, I'd like to give a special thanks to all of my family and friends who supported me in any way during this process. Also, to family members who watched me write during family visits on both the Thanksgiving and Christmas holidays, thank you.

I want to thank my editor, Miranda Henley, again, for your patience, skill, and great work.

I want to recognize all of my former teams and teammates. Wonder Jr. High in West Memphis, Arkansas, where it all started—middle-school football with Coach Bowens and Coach Ball, two of the best. To all of my former teammates from Wonder Jr. High "Lions"—respect. A special thanks to coach Willie Bowens, my Algebra teacher and first-ever football coach (brilliant mind), who taught me to be a student athlete.

Recognition to all of my former teammates and coaches from West Memphis High School—respect. *Go, Blue Devils!* Also to the University of Arkansas Razorbacks football program, and to all of my former teammates—respect. Also one of the best freshman classes of the 1987 college football season.

Recognition to all of my former teammates and coaches from the University of Memphis Tigers (Memphis State University)—respect. Some of the more fun, most colorful characters ever, even to this day—what up "South Hall." I also want to recognize all University of Memphis Alumni.

To all of my former teammates and coaches from the Cleveland Browns—respect. A special thanks to my former trainer Bill Tessendorf and Dr. Bergfeld who tried everything possible to save my career. To the

Browns organization, forever first class, and the die-hard Browns fan base—one of the best in the league; and to the City of Cleveland—respect.

Finally, to all of my former teammates and coaches from the New Orleans Saints; we had some great times and made some history together (first Saints team to win an NFC West Championship, #1 Defense and #1 Pass Defense). To all of my Saints alum—respect. I want to recognize the Saints organization, and the most colorful, most jazzy and best dancing fans in the entire league—the Saints fans. The City of New Orleans is like a second home to me—what a great comeback story: New Orleans, Louisiana.

I've been truly blessed to have been a part of so many great teams and to have had so many great teammates—for that I'm grateful.

Author's Note

*F*irst and foremost, I want to start by expressing my deepest gratitude and saying thank you to every single reader who picks up this book and makes a purchase. Also, thank you to every reader who shares this book or information about this book with anyone else. A special thanks to every reader who shares this book with family and friends around the world via social media.

I made every effort to write this book where it wasn't too technical for a novice or too boring for a reader who has some base knowledge of the game. As a result, I intentionally avoided writing about Xs and Os. I also avoided writing about penalties and rules due to the fact that some of the rules are subject to change year after year. Also, I made every effort to make this book relevant for women who would like to get a feel for American football decades from now.

It's been an extremely exciting and challenging journey; I started this project on January 1, 2012, with a goal to finish it January 1, 2013. As a result of my determination to realize my goal, I found myself getting an average of three hours of sleep per night for the last five months of this project. I'm more than happy to have paid the price, and I'm very proud to have realized that goal

This book encompasses well over 20 years of passion and studying the game of American football. The motivation to write was both to share my passion and to help the masses of women who are interested in learning about and getting a feel for the game.

I would also like for this book to serve as a form of encouragement and inspiration for any reader who has ever abruptly lost something dear or had a passion taken away. I, like many other former NFL players, had to make the difficult transition from the game and from my passion for playing the game. Although I've long gotten over the desire to play the game, this book is a comeback project for me; I always want to be a part of the game in some way.

Remember to never give up on your dreams. You may have to reinvent yourself, but don't ever give up on your dreams. Stay tuned: That's the theme of next book—a game plan to realize your dreams.

I find it most rewarding to help others learn this great game of American football.

Again, valued reader, thank you very much!

Contents

Introduction

$\mathcal{A}$merican football is a gender-neutral sport. This book is about looking at American football from the portrayal of a former professional football player and about how the game can be simplified when you parallel it to everyday relationships.

The intention of this book is not to highlight the complexity of the game, nor is it to tutor you in order for you to achieve the highest football IQ. The purpose is to simplify diverse components and concepts and ultimately give you a great feel for the game. Please relax and enjoy your new sense of understanding and appreciation for the game as you view American football from the acumen of a former NFL player.

You don't need to know as much as the paid professionals who play the game. But wouldn't it be cool—wouldn't it help you as a follower—to not be turned off by the complexity of comprehension and instead have a satisfying feel for the game?

Let me be clear: Regarding the antiquated attitude of men who still think and argue that American football is a man's game, I'm here to bring you up-to-date—American football is no longer branded as male-oriented. Ask the National Football League; they have created and sell female apparel as a result of their extensive female fan base. In addition, the female fan base is significant in high-school football and college football.

Although the overall mission of this book is not intended to debunk the stereotype that women are not football fans, the fact of the matter is, the gridiron (the football field) is and has been officially gender-neutral for some time now. Ladies, for those of you who are new to the game, welcome; and for those who already follow, continue to enjoy the game—it's a great game. I love this game!

This book is designed to help you comprehend the many facets of American football, as well as help you circumvent any confusion you feel, perhaps because you've been told how complex the game really is—or because you've simply been told zilch. Often, those you would like to ask, or those you would like to bond with around this game, simply will not answer any football questions during a game, or in some cases, will not answer any football questions at all during the season.

I will answer many of the questions you have about American football; I will show you how to interpret the various nuances and different facets of the game. In this book, I make every effort to talk to you, just as I would if I were sitting with you face-to-face and coaching you on the game.

This book will make football matters simpler and lay out a straightforward path you can follow. If you have a limited understanding of the game or no knowledge at all, you will find that this book can help you eliminate any stress you may feel regarding the intricacies of the game and help you form a framework of understanding so you feel in control.

This book is written with several groups of women in mind. One group is little-league football moms. Your little kid is about to embark upon a sport that is demanding, physical, and challenging to understand. You will gain a better understanding by reading this book.

To middle-school football moms and high-school football moms, maybe you've followed your son as he's played this sport for a while now. You feel comfortable that you understand a little bit about the basics, but you would like to know a lot more. This book will help expand your perception of the game.

I've also created this book with high-school football cheerleaders, college football cheerleaders/dancers, and professional football cheerleaders/dancers in mind. You love cheering and dancing for your respective teams, and you enjoy the games. However, you don't always "get" the sport. And maybe you're even frustrated because you think the game is too confusing, and you've given up on understanding very much beyond a first down and a touchdown. This book will simplify things.

Likewise, for female college students—perhaps your roommate, boyfriend, and/or sororities are big supporters of your college football team. And although you generally tag along, you simply don't have a clue as to what's going on during the course of a game. After reading this book, you will gain a good feel for the game and will no longer be the one wondering what happened when the crowd erupts in cheers or frenzy.

This book is also for women who are intrigued with American football. Maybe you admire the game from a distance or even from another country, but you've never taken the time to embrace it. Perhaps you're now at a state where you're very curious. Your curiosity will be addressed in the book, and you'll be able to appreciate the game with a good understanding.

Additionally, I've written this for women who want to bond with partners, spouses, or loved ones who are totally hooked on American football, especially college football and professional football. Reading this book will help you better comprehend and appreciate the game, and hopefully, your loved ones will appreciate your commitment to learning more. Your newfound feel for the game will allow you the ability to stay connected to or bond with your significant other or loved ones more during the six months of football fever.

And, of course, I've written this book for women who follow the NFL and would simply like to have a better grasp of the game. Perhaps you are a new follower or you have followed for a while and have made good strides in understanding the game. However, you would like to make greater gains. By reading this book, you will score in comprehension.

The organization of this book is simple; I take you through the process of seeing and feeling the game of American football from the viewpoint of relationships. In the spirit of full disclosure, I am not a relationship expert, do not claim to be, nor do I intend to be—I am not striving to be, nor do I dream to be. I write metaphorically from my opinions about relationships. I divide the book into three "Phases" for ease and continuity.

Phase I details the organization and schemes within the framework of an American football team, as well as the three teams within the overall team structure. Phase II illustrates the process of how teammates coexist and communicate. Phase III introduces ideas that are essential for understanding key components of the game. I encourage you to read this book in its three Phases. The three Phases are as follows: Phase I—Chapters 1, 2, 3, and 4; Phase II—Chapters 5 and 6; and Phase III—Chapters 7, 8, and 9.

While this book is written with women as the central focus, I presume that there will be some men who don't follow American football and have never learned the game who will be interested in reading it. (In fact, one of my good friends, an Italian physician and researcher, has assured me that he will be the first one to read the book.) Men, by all means, please enjoy the read.

But once again, the heart of the matter is helping women to get a feel for the game. Ladies, please join me in this excursion on the gridiron.

Phase 1

Chapter 1

Team

Relationships

A team is a collage of talents, personalities, and alliances—a collage comprised of goals, strategy, skill, effort, roles, unity, and will. "The sum of us is greater than all our parts" is not simply a beautiful cliché but also a fundamental requirement for successful teams. Joint effort and synergy are the heartbeat of a team.

The adage that there is strength in numbers holds especially true when you build strong and strategic alliances. With others, certainly we can accomplish more. An ancient philosophy says that two are better than one because they reward each other for their efforts. And if they fail, one will lift up his equal (teammate). Similarly, as another adage puts it, "A threefold cord is not quickly broken," meaning simply that we are stronger when we band together as one.

When individuals partner in a relationship, they form a *team*. Indeed, relationships are similar to an American football team. It's imperative for all of the parties involved to recognize that the dynamics of the team are exceptionally important.

In a similar fashion, you can appreciate your own talents and values, as well as the talents and values of your partner, or in the case of a football team—your teammate. On a football team, a football player has defined roles and responsibilities. The same can be said of relationship teams. Cultivating teamwork builds relationships that value **team spirit**.

Teams best exemplify the framework of a unit working simultaneously to reach a common goal. In order for a player to demonstrate *team spirit*, he has to make his individual goal(s) immaterial. The primary objective must be to obtain the **team goals**. And each individual accomplishment comes as a result of this unified pursuit of the *team goals*.

Football teams and relationship teams are comparable in that they both take time to build trust and unity. In due course, both also require an enormous amount of practice to accomplish this trust and unity. Relationship teams embody a type of *team spirit* when both members see their individual goals as not significant in relation to their overall *team goals* (for the relationship team).

And just as relationship teams can benefit from defining each member's roles and expectations, and avoiding guessing games, it's very important that players' roles and expectations be defined. Otherwise, insecurity and disarray will impede the team's goals.

We know that any relationship team will experience ups and downs. Football teams also face adversity and have their own ups and downs. And as with relationship teams, working collectively through tough times will make football teams stronger. Football teams that succeed are battle-tested; if you contrast any successful relationship team, it too will prove to be battle-tested. Joint effort and synergy create a winner.

An American football team is made up of three teams in one: the **offensive team**, the **defensive team**, and the **special teams**. The amount of **talent** and the makeup of *talent* a football team has are essential to the success of the team. In the makeup of *talent*, football teams have both **role players** and **star players**.

The majority of every American football team is made up of *role players*. A *role player* is very comfortable in his skin and with his role on the team as a teammate and contributor. He is not attracted to the spotlight of stardom and is very content to bask in the glow and glory of the team's success. There are *role players* on all three units: *the offensive team, the defensive team*, and *the special teams*.

One example of a *role player* is a **fullback**. A *fullback* is one of the **running backs**—he is the *running back* who blocks for the **halfback**, or **tailback**. The terminology differs depending on the team. The *halfback*, or *tailback*, gets to carry/run the football often and, in many cases, will have the opportunity to score touchdowns. In many instances, when a *halfback* (H-back) is really good, he is probably one of the *star players* on the team. Now, on the other hand, the *fullback* on most football teams very rarely gets to carry/run the football. Consequently, the *fullback* rarely scores a touchdown. The primary responsibility of the *fullback* on most football teams is to block and take punishment for the *halfback*. This *fullback* is a *role player* on most football teams and is very proud of his role; he takes great pride in performing well.

The **star player** is the player who's expected to shine every game. The *star player* is a game changer—on any play, he can do something spectacular that can change the outcome of the game. He is an impact player—expected to deliver during crunch time, when the game is on the line. So, naturally, he gets all of the media hype, as well as the big money, in the case of professional football.

In most cases, the **quarterback**, **running back**, and **receiver** are *star players* on the *offensive team*; on the *defensive team*, the *star players* can vary from **linebackers** to a **defensive back**, and so on.

Although, not every *role player* is a *star player*, every *star player* is a *role player*.

Contrary to the belief of some *star players* and some **selfish players**, no football team can win on the success of any one *star player* alone. It will always take some blocking, running, passing, kicking, catching and tackling to get the job done. There is no one player who can do all of these things over the course of a game. A win is always a *team* effort in an American football game, especially in the NFL.

There is no shortage of **personalities** on every football team. I will highlight a few. . . .

The **confident player** is a player who is always sure that his hard work, combined with his talent(s), ensures him a good performance every time he takes the football field. The *confident player* is self-assured in his knowledge of the playbook as it pertains to executing assignments applicable to his position and role on the team. The *confident player* doesn't fear his opponent because he knows that he can compete with anyone as long as he prepares properly. The *confident player* knows that actions speak louder than words. The *confident player* has confidence in his coach, and he trusts the system.

Contrast the **cocky player**, who proclaims execution before it ever exists. The *cocky player* boasts his performance as a prelude to the actual game. According to the *cocky player*, there is nothing he cannot do. In his mind, he is the jack-of-all-trades, yet he actually masters none. The *cocky player* is always critical of his teammates' performances and is rarely supportive. So it begs the question, Is the *cocky player* over-compensating verbally for his physical shortcomings? I've always seen the *cocky player* as having a small-confidence complex. The *cocky player* has a distorted view that his words express as a tangible form of action.

Over the course of every game, there are a number of players who get knocked on their butts time after time. However, the **tenacious player** will get up and continue to compete over and over again. Also, there is the **timid player**; after he gets knocked on his butt really hard a couple of times, he experiences what I refer to as getting his **manhood minimized**. He goes into a timid state and hides in a shell for the remainder of the game. For the *timid player*, getting his *manhood minimized* means that his competitiveness has been reduced—totally minimized after this stage—for the duration of the game.

The *tenacious player* simply has a get-back-up-again attitude and a never-quit mentality. The *tenacious player* believes the philosophy that you don't quit until the last whistle has blown and all of the time has expired on the game clock. The *tenacious player* accepts the fact that if you continue to compete on each and every play, even when things aren't going well, eventually something good with happen for you.

The *timid player* rarely realizes his full potential because he's usually not willing to endure adversity. The *timid player* is up one moment, then down another because he has a **fragile confidence**, which means that, in the face of adversity, his confidence is subject to break. The *timid player* is willing to terminate the mission, but the *tenacious player* is determined to execute the team goals at all costs.

There is an interesting facet to the physical game of American football. So many players give the appearance of the macho-man mentality, yet they play with such a *fragile confidence* and occasionally experience what I call the **long-face syndrome**. The *long-face syndrome* is when a player makes a mistake or a really bad play and then wears his emotions on his face. It takes some players longer than others to get over their mistakes. Over the course of a game, you can see multiple players on either team exhibit the *long-face syndrome*. I think it's safe to say that men are emotional. It's also safe to conclude that American football is an emotional game.

This *long-face syndrome* is even more evident with **kickers** and *quarterbacks*. When a *kicker* misses an easy field goal attempt or misses a potential game-winning field goal, quite often he will keep his helmet on—to deal with the *long-face syndrome*. Similarly, when *quarterbacks* make a good play and go to the sidelines, they normally take off their helmets and put on a cap—they show their happy faces. Quite the opposite is true when they make a mistake or a really bad play. In many of these situations, you will see the *quarterback* leave his helmet on and maybe just stand on the sideline instead of sitting on the bench with his cap on. He will keep his helmet on, and you can still see his distress as he displays the *long-face syndrome*.

This is rather remarkable because there are instances when a *quarterback* does not complete a comeback attempt or the *quarterback* makes a play that costs his team the game—you will certainly see the *long-face syndrome* on display. Again, you might even see the *quarterback* keep his helmet on as he goes to the locker room, defeated and dejected, with the *long-face syndrome*.

There are football players who are cool and calm in pressure situations—the saying is, "They have ice-water running through their veins." Then, there are other players who crack or blow up under pressure; they become overwhelmed. There's a saying that players like to use for players who blow up under pressure: "Pressure will bust a pipe."

There are number of **alliances** formed on every football team. There are *alliances* between players and coaches, as well as between players and their teammates. Quite often, coaches form *alliances* with their *team leaders* and *team captains*. There are many examples of *alliances* between players and their teammates; running backs form *alliances* with offensive linemen, quarterbacks form *alliances* with receivers, quarterbacks form *alliances* with offensive linemen, linebackers form *alliances* with defensive linemen, and defensive safeties form *alliances* with defensive cornerbacks, etc.

Although, I had great *alliances* with most of my coaches over the years, in one instance, I had one of my coaches try to form an *alliance* with me at the beginning of a new season. Normally, I got along great with all of my coaches and respected all of them—from middle-school football all the way through professional football. However, this particular coach made a move to establish his *alliance* with me in a team meeting in front of everyone on the team. While that in and of itself was not problematic, the problem with this setup was that he did it immediately after he had just blasted one of my defensive teammates in front of the entire team. The coach took about five minutes berating my teammate—he not only wanted this player to know that his attitude and effort were not good enough, but he also wanted to express his opinion to the team that this particular teammate was a loser.

So after that, the coach decided to transition to me as an example— I was team captain, model citizen, and as he explained, I worked hard on every play in practice; I had laser focus, and I was a smart player and a student of the game—all great compliments. Then, in an effort to pivot in order to establish and solidify an *alliance* with me, he yelled out, "Reggie, do you love football?"

Now, hold the press—this particular coach had no idea that I was troubled and disappointed at the way he had just stripped down my teammate's ego and embarrassed him profusely in front of the entire team. This team captain was not prepared to affirm this *alliance*. So, the coach yelled again, boldly and loudly, as I had not yet responded, "Reggie, do you love football?"

I intentionally paused, as if maybe I hadn't heard him the first two times; so he asked a third time—"Reggie, do you love football?"

I was still not prepared to endorse that character assignation, nor this *alliance* under these circumstances. So, I responded with the best poker face and in the most monotone expression possible—"I . . . like . . . football." Note: I absolutely love football and absolutely loved football at the time; however, I just could not endorse him in that situation.

My teammates knew that I was a team player, and if any *alliance* was affirmed that day, the *alliance* with my teammates was reaffirmed. My teammates spoke of that incident throughout the entire season, with enormous amusement and pride.

When you build an *alliance* with the vision, values, and core competencies of your teammates, their goals become your goals and vice versa. The goals become a **mutual mission**. When you understand who your teammate(s) or partner(s) are and what they would like to accomplish, then you begin to help each other realize your goals. You create an *alliance* that will always support one another. This team-building framework for football teams seems as though it would work for relationship teams as well.

As a defensive cornerback in the NFL, I formed alliances with defensive linemen on our team. I would cook for three of our defensive linemen and invite them to my house for dinner once a month. This was a fun and productive time with regards to forming *alliances*.

I also formed *alliances* with all of the defensive backs. When I played with the New Orleans Saints, all of the defensive backs, safeties, and cornerbacks would meet once a week—every Monday or Tuesday evening; a handful of the defensive backs, who had ulterior motives, chose a certain establishment for us to meet. Now, their claim was that they merely enjoyed eating the wings and were not necessarily focused on observing the assets that were on display at this establishment. Nevertheless, by meeting and hanging out away from the locker room, meeting room, and practice field, we built some really strong *alliances*.

In some instances, a football team may be struggling to have consistent success in winning games, but their *alliance* is so strong they feel like it's them against the world; they take on the *us against them* mentality. This understanding and *alliance* with vision, values, and goals, produces a strong and resilient bond that is very essential to building **team unity**.

There is a **mutual mission** when a coach is able to bring together all of the team's *talents*, *personalities*, and *alliances* in an effort to embrace and advance the team goals. In a *mutual mission*, players are prepared to commit their *talents* to the mission of the team. Players also surrender their individualities for the identity of the team. The various *alliances* that are formed on a team are an integral part of the mutual mission, moving it forward. Each player must be on the same page as both his teammates and his coaches.

Coaches establish an *alliance* with their **team captain(s)** and star players to develop the type of *team culture* they desire. There are two primary areas of focus in terms of developing *team culture*: the **meeting room** and the **practice field**.

Players who are committed to advancing goals are attentive in the *team meetings*, remain alert during film study, and work hard on the *practice field*. These players are committed both mentally and physically.

On the other side, players who impede goals are not attentive in *team meetings*, find time to nap in film study, and for some reason, choose not to work hard on every play on the *practice field*. This kind of preparation won't help—it can only hinder execution and ultimately impede team goals. Players who impede goals are not usually bothered by losing games, as long as they play well and/or look good. These players care more about playing time than they do about winning.

Team culture reflects the beliefs, habits, and values that a football team maintains in order to realize their *team goals*. Again, the two primary areas of focus with regards to developing *team culture* are the *meeting rooms* and the *practice field*.

The **meeting rooms** are where the football team meets to discuss their goals, strategy, and opponents. They also watch films of their previous game, their practices during the week of preparation for their upcoming opponents, and their upcoming opponents' previous games.

In American football, especially in college football and professional football, football teams meet as a group in a **team meeting**. They also meet as individual teams: **offensive team meeting**, (the entire *offensive team* meets), **defensive team meeting** (the entire defensive team meets), and **special teams meeting** (all of the *special teams* meet).

In addition to the *team meeting*, *offensive team meeting*, *defensive team meeting*, and *special teams meeting*, players have meetings according to their different positions. For example, the *offensive team* breakdown: *running backs meeting, quarterbacks meeting, receivers meeting*, and *offensive-line meeting*. Likewise, the defensive team breakdown: *defensive linemen meeting, linebackers meeting*, and *defensive backs meeting*. Also, there's a breakdown with the *special teams*; some teams have meetings with all of that *special team*'s players, while others may break them up: *punt team and punt-return team meeting, kickoff team and kickoff-return team meeting*, and *kickers and holders meeting*.

The bulk of the time that players spend in the *meeting room* is by position and with their position coaches. Again, the players spend some of their time in team meetings, where the head coach discusses the overall team goals and the overall team strategy. And the players also spend some time in the individual team meetings. For example, in the *offensive team meeting*, the offensive team will discuss in more detail their goals and strategy regarding their upcoming opponents' defensive team. Similarly, in the *defensive team meeting*, the defensive team will discuss in more detail their goals and strategy regarding their upcoming opponents' offensive team. And so on, with the *special teams meeting*.

In the **position meetings**, not only do the position coaches and players discuss in even more detail their position goals and strategy regarding their upcoming opponents, but they also watch films of their opponents' previous games.

A fascinating afterthought regarding meeting rooms: Some teams have more players who fall asleep in the meeting rooms than others. Now, the players who fall asleep in the meeting rooms are very strategic. By this, I mean that they wouldn't dare fall asleep in the team meeting because the team meeting is executed by the head football coach. Certainly, if the **head coach** caught a player asleep in the team meeting, the consequences would be severe. Also, the players are just as careful not to fall asleep in the offensive team meeting or defensive team meeting, since the **offensive coordinator / defensive coordinator** (the coach who directs and manages the entire offensive / defensive team) would also issue out serious consequences if he caught a player sleeping during the meeting.

So, the players wait to sneak and take their naps in the position meeting for two reasons. One, they know that they are going to be in the position meeting for the longest amount of time—these meetings provide more of an opportunity, and these sleepers are opportunists. Second, they know their position coach is not as commanding and tends to be more lenient than the *head coach* and *coordinators*. Keep in mind, this is a small number of players. Still, there's a lot of snoozing going on in many of the position meetings, especially in the NFL.

Some players go hard every play, every day on the practice field. There are other players who not only take certain plays off in practice but also take certain days off, where they do not go hard on every play on the practice field. Some players just simply do not focus or work hard in practice. They are the type of players who think they can chill on the practice field and just turn it on for game day. This arrogance does not work and always leads to poor execution on game day.

When I played, I took great pride in the fact that I knew I was blessed with exceptional talent. Therefore, I always wanted to go the extra mile and work hard to perfect my skills. If you were to question any of my former teammates, from my middle-school football team, high-school football team, college football team, or professional football team, you would be hard-pressed to find a single former teammate who would say that I didn't work extremely hard on the practice field, every play, every day of my career.

Some players don't appreciate the old saying, "Preparation time is never wasted time," or the one that says, "Practice makes perfect." Absolutely, great practices do perfect execution.

One day after a practice during my third season in the NFL, my head coach told me that he wanted to meet me in his office. I was curious—I had not gotten into any trouble, so I didn't have a clue what this meeting was going to be about. When I got to my coach's office and sat down in front of him, he explained that he was pleased with my progress since I had been with the team and that I had really great work ethic. He said he wanted me to, and would be expecting me to, step up this season and be one of the *leaders* on the defensive team. Then he asked if I was comfortable with taking on that role. I said sure I would; however, I would probably *lead by example* more often and occasionally be a *verbal leader*. He said that was fine, but that he wanted me to be sure to be a *verbal leader* at times as well.

During the time I had accepted this role as one of the *leaders* on the defensive team, I often dreamed of our team winning a Super Bowl—receiving a Super Bowl ring and getting a trip to 1600 Pennsylvania Avenue to meet and be honored by the President of the United States. Unfortunately, multiple knee surgeries ended my NFL career sooner than anticipated, and I never realized those dreams. So, I guess what's left of that dream is that maybe I'll still have the opportunity one day to meet the President of the United States.

There are the two types of **leaders** on an American football team. There are players who **lead by example**; they work really hard, and they know their playbook so well that they are also able to assist their teammates if necessary. They sit up front in the meeting room and will occasionally ask questions to get an emphasis on something they think might benefit their teammates; they never fall asleep in the meeting rooms. They are the first on the practice field and the last to leave it, and nobody on the team works harder than they do on the practice field.

The other type of *leader* is a **verbal leader**; this is a leader who works really hard too, but they are far more verbal than the players who *lead by* *example*. The *verbal leader* does both really well; they *lead by example* and motivate their teammates every time they speak. The attitude and actions of players and coaches in the meeting rooms and on the practice field is the staple of *team culture*, and *team leaders* can help develop and influence that *team culture*.

Every *leader* on a football team is not always one of the *team captains*; however, every *team captain* is a *leader*. Although I was not a *team captain* when I played in the NFL, I was a *team leader*. I always loved to *lead by example*.

There are two notable players on an American football team: the **team player** and the **selfish player**. You can distinguish a *team player* from a *selfish player* by whether the player is focused on **self-improvement** or **self-promotion**. The *team player* is dedicated, humble, and reliable. The *selfish player* is self-indulgent, egotistical, and narcissistic. The best comparison for the *selfish player*: He is like a gold-digger. He certainly cares more about the money than the *mission*—it's all about the gold, not the goals; he champions the treasure, not the team.

There is usually an enormous amount of talk from *selfish players* around "I." It's either in the form of "I" did this or "I" did that; "I" don't do this or "I" don't do that. Either way it's presented, it comes down to *self-promotion*. Generally speaking, *selfish players* are so consumed with *self-promotion* that they don't have a real concept of the team philosophy—let alone *team spirit*.

Team players always focus on *self-improvement* because they are most concerned with how to enhance their roles as *team players*—to increase the overall success of the team. *Self-improvement* is more in line with the *team spirit* than *self-promotion*. *Self-improvement* boosts the team's goals, and *self-promotion* boosts the agenda of the *selfish player*.

The distinction between the *team players* and the *selfish players* is crystal clear. Because the *team players* are focused on *self-improvement*, they do things for the good of the team, embrace the "we" syndrome (they refer to themselves as part of the team), and are committed contributors. On the other hand, the *selfish players* are focused on *self-promotion*, and they do things for the good of themselves; they embrace the "me" syndrome and are like an uncommitted gold-digger. (In addition, they often like to refer to themselves in the third person.)

In order to accomplish overall *team goals*, *self-improvement* by each player on the team has to take precedence over *self-promotion*, just as with relationships. Similar to football teams, relationship teams are adversely impacted when either member champions *self-promotion* over *self*-improvement. Relationship teams are on the right track to realize *team goals* when each member makes *self-improvement* a priority.

When all three units on an American football team work as one, it creates a threefold cord that's not easily broken. *Team unity* in action—the *us against them* mentality—demonstrates that we win together and we lose together. The offensive team, defensive team, and special teams each have specific goals for their units; however, the basis of those goals is dedicated to the mission of the overall team goals.

Although the overall team goals are more important than any player's individual goals, each of the individual teams' goals (meaning the *offensive team*, *defensive team*, and *special teams*) are consistent with realizing the overall team goals. What's essential with regards to each of the three teams is that each one contributes something in terms of positive production, each and every game. This contribution does not always and will not in many cases be equal; nevertheless, there has to be some contribution in order for the football team to win games on a regular basis.

Similarly, relationship teams benefit when each member has some contribution on a regular basis.

Team players are the key contributors on both football teams and relationship teams. *Team goals* are what drive both football teams and relationship teams to achieve success together. *Team spirit* is the support mechanism for football teams and relationship teams. *Team culture* is the value system for both football teams and relationship teams. *Team unity* is the lifeblood of football teams and relationship teams. Joint effort and synergy are the heartbeat of both football teams and relationship teams.

CHAPTER 2

Offensive Team

Finesse

*T*he **offensive team** is expected to be the **point producers**. The scheme or system that *offensive teams* use to score points varies greatly from team to team, as well as from coach to coach. The plan of attack of most *offensive teams* contrasts greatly from that of *defensive teams*. Most defensive teams take on more of a physical posture, meaning that most of what they design and do is centered on being more physical than their opponents' offensive teams.

On the other hand, many *offensive teams* take on more of a finesse attitude. They will rely on a collection of schemes, a selection of skilled players, and a range of strategies to try to outsmart their opponents' defensive teams.

In American football there are 11 players from each team on the football field all of the time. When the offensive team is on the field with their 11 offensive players, the opponents' defensive team is on the field with their 11 defensive players. It's always 11 against 11.

Let's meet the 11 players that represent the *offensive team*:

The **quarterback** (QB) is the leader on the offensive team. His is usually the most touted and most recognized position on the field. The *quarterback* (QB) is the player who throws the football to the receivers, tight ends, and running backs; he also hands off the football to running backs.

The *quarterback* (QB) is generally one of the star players for almost all teams—even on losing teams. The *quarterback*, by virtue of his position, is the offensive team leader and a verbal leader. He is also called the **signal caller** or **field general**. The quarterbacks' (QB) position coach is called a **quarterbacks coach**.

Offensive linemen (OL) are usually the largest players on the offensive team; these players provide protection (blocking) for the quarterback, running backs, and receivers. The role of an *offensive lineman* (OL) is to block the opponents' *defensive linemen*. Individual offensive line positions include: center (C), left guard (LG), left tackle (LT), right guard (RG), and right tackle (RT). Generally in American football, there are at least five *offensive linemen* (OL) on each offensive play.

Let's take a closer look at the **offensive line** (OL):

The **center** (C) is located in the middle of the *offensive line*. This is the player who **snaps** the football; *Snapping* is when the *center* (C) moves the football from its position on the field and passes it between his legs into the hands of the *quarterback* (QB), who is standing behind him. The communication between the *center* (C) and the *quarterback* (QB) is extremely important because these are the two players who initiate almost all offensive plays from the **line of scrimmage** (the location on the football field where the football is placed and all plays are initiated) with the process of *snapping* the football.

There's a **verbal exchange** and a **physical exchange** between the quarterback (QB) and the center (C) on every offensive play. The *verbal exchange* is the communication from the quarterback (QB) in the huddle regarding what the **snap count** is (which command or number the quarterback (QB) has told the center (C) to *snap* or give him the football in order to initiate the play from the *line of scrimmage*; for example, it can be on one, two, or three, etc.). This *verbal exchange* continues at the *line of scrimmage* when the quarterback (QB) and center (C) actually execute the *snap* to start the play. There's also a *physical exchange*—when the football is exchanged from the center (C) to the quarterback (QB).

The **guards** (G) are positioned on both sides of the center (C)—**left guard** (LG) and **right guard** (RG). The *left guard* (LG) lines up to the left of the center (C). The *right guard* (RG) lines up to the right of the center (C). In most cases, the *guards* are role players; occasionally, there's a guard who's so outstanding that he becomes a star player.

The **tackles** are positioned on each side of the guards—**left tackle** (LT) and **right tackle** (RT). The *left tackle* (LT) lines up next to the left guard (LG), and the *right tackle* (RT) lines up next to the right guard (RG). In most cases, the *tackles* are role players. Note: The *left tackle* is generally the most esteemed of all of the five offensive linemen because he protects the quarterback's (QB) blindside (backside)—most quarterbacks (QB) are right-handed, and when they drop back for a pass, they cannot see a rushing defender coming from their blindside. For this reason, the *left tackle* (LT) will always be a high-value player.

When the offensive team is on the football field, there is always a *center* (C), two *guards* (G), and two *tackles* (T); this represents the *offensive line*.

(LT–LG–C–RG–RT)

The offensive line (OL) position coach is called the **offensive line coach** or **O-line coach**. In many instances, the *O-line coach* is one of the most intense coaches on the team.

A **tight end** (TE) has the dual role of blocking for the running backs (RB) on running plays and catching passes from the quarterback (QB) on passing plays. Depending on the team and the team's strategy, a *tight end* (TE) functions primarily like another offensive lineman, or for some teams, he functions primarily as a *receiver*. In most cases, the *tight end* (TE) is a role player; occasionally, in particular in the NFL, a few teams will highlight the *tight end* (TE). Consequently, the *tight end* (TE) in this scenario is a star player.

Tight ends line up beside the tackles on either side of the football. There are different times when an offensive team will have one or two *tight ends* on the football field, and there are other times when the offensive team will not have any *tight ends* (TEs) on the field. The *tight ends'* (TEs) position coach is called the **tight ends coach**.

Receivers (WR) can function as *wide receivers* and *slot receivers*. A **wide receiver** (WR) is the primary target for an offensive team for most passing plays in the passing game. The *wide receiver* (WR) is usually highly skilled and usually possesses a lot of speed. In most cases, the *receivers* (WRs) are the players on the team who are the very best at catching the football. The job of a *wide receiver* (WR) is to have success against the defensive backs—in most cases, the defensive cornerback (CB). In many instances, one of the *receivers* is a star player, and generally the rest of the *receivers* are role players. *Receivers* (WRs) line up outside of the tackles (RT, LT) or tight ends (TEs) on either side of the football, oftentimes near the sideline. The *receivers* run down the field and catch the football, normally thrown to them by the quarterback (QB)—there is an occasional pass thrown by a halfback (HB) or *wide receiver* (WR). When two *wide receivers* (WRs) line up on the same side of the football, the receiver on the inside is referred to as the **slot receiver**. *Receivers'* (WRs) position coach is called a **receivers coach**.

The **running back** (RB) takes the football from the quarterback (this is a handoff) and runs with it; his primary role is to carry/run the football, with the aim of gaining territory and scoring in the running game. The *running back* often lines up directly behind the quarterback (QB), and sometimes behind the quarterback (QB) to the left or right.

Occasionally a *running back* (RB) will function as a *receiver* out of the backfield, as well as occasionally block on passing plays. Most offensive teams will typically have a star player for one of their *running backs* (RBs), and the rest of the players in the group are generally role players. Depending on the offensive formation (arrangement/positioning of the offensive players), a *running back* is a *halfback* (HB), *tailback* (TB), or *fullback* (FB). *Running backs'* (RB) position coach is called a **running backs coach**.

Note: Each offensive team can use any variation of personnel they choose, based on their schemes and strategies. For example, on certain plays, an offensive team may have only one running back in the game, or two tight ends, or four receivers, etc.

The offensive team uses what's called **situational preparation** (planning and preparing for different situations by studying the opponents' personnel and tendencies) to prepare for their opponents' defensive team. Usually, the offensive team prepares from two perspectives—one is based on the offensive team's philosophy, strengths, and game plan.

Secondly, the offensive team prepares for their opponents' defensive team based on what the defensive team's strengths and weaknesses are, as well as whether their defensive team takes a conservative approach or an aggressive approach. *Situational preparation* is done in the form of studying and reviewing the opponents' personnel and tendencies (what type of plays they run, when they like to run what play, and where on the field and how often they like to run certain defensive plays). In *situational preparation*, the offensive team tries to prepare for every possible situation and scenario they may encounter against the opponents' defensive team.

The team player always takes *situational preparation* seriously, with a concentrated focus and an intense attention to details—unlike the selfish player who has a fickle focus and is often detached when it comes to attention to details. Again, the selfish player is on and off with regards to preparation because he takes both his opponent and preparation lightly.

The **offensive game plan** is the part of the coaches' overall game plan specifically designed as a plan of attack for the offensive team against the opponents' defensive team.

An *offensive game plan* is usually a plan of attack designed with a strategy for utilizing both the running game and the passing game. One coach will choose a *conservative approach* with their passing game and an *aggressive approach* with their running game, while another coach may have an *offensive game plan* that calls for an *aggressive approach* in the passing game and a *conservative approach* in the running game. Then, there's another coach who has an *offensive game plan* where he chooses a **balanced attack**, which depends on both the running game and the passing game equally.

Some teams' *offensive game plans* will call for the offensive team to execute to perfection four to five plays they can run over and over. In order to disguise these repetitive tactics, some coaches will run the same four to five plays in a different formation (how the offensive team lines up at the *line of scrimmage*) or alignment. Sometimes the coach will run the same plays, with a player in motion (when the offensive team moves one of their players, running from one side of the field to the other before the football is *snapped*; this motion normally takes place behind the quarterback (QB) and offensive linemen (OL).

Coaches can be described as having a **conservative approach** or an **aggressive approach** to coaching during games. There are several ways to determine which category a coach falls into:

- One way a coach is described as having a **conservative approach** is by the ratio of running plays to passing plays he calls throughout the course of a game. For example, a coach who takes a *conservative approach* may call 40 running plays and 20 passing plays in a game where his offensive team has a total of 60 offensive plays. Contrast that with the coach who takes an **aggressive approach**; similarly, the offensive team for this coach has 60 total offensive plays over the course of a game, and the coach calls 40 passing plays and 20 running plays.
- Coaches who take a conservative approach simply do not like to take very many risks, if any at all, during the course of a game—especially in situations where there is a need to gain a lot of yards in order to get or secure a 1st down. (Generally, when you need 10 yards or more on a 3rd-down situation, it is considered a lot.) Note: An offensive team is allowed 4 downs (1st down, 2nd down, 3rd down, and 4th down), or 4 attempts to gain a total of 10 yards, which constitutes getting or securing a 1st down/1st & 10.
- An additional characteristic that distinguishes a *conservative approach* versus an *aggressive approach* is whether the coach is willing to take a chance on long field goal (FG) attempts when the field

goal (FG) kicker would be making an attempt on the very edge of his actual kicking range (the farthest distance he has successfully made a field goal (FG) in previous games). The dilemma in this case is that if the field goal kicker misses a long field goal, especially in a close game, it will leave the opponents' offensive team with great field position, thereby putting the opponents' offensive team in a position to have a high probability of moving into a scoring position.

- Another possible determination is dealing with a 4th-down scenario. Generally speaking, a coach who takes a conservative approach will almost never take a chance on a 4th down or the 4th attempt, even in cases where the offensive team only needs to gain 1 yard or even a half of a yard in order to get a 1st down (1st & 10).
- It could also be determined by whether a coach is willing to take a chance on 4th & goal (4th down from the goal line), with a chance to score a touchdown versus attempting a field goal.

Most offensive teams usually run most of their favorite plays out of their playbook when they have good **field position**. Note, *field position* is a huge factor for calling offensive plays. Good *field position* gives offensive coaches the freedom to utilize their full selection of plays, whereas bad *field position* limits play calling.

The **down** that an offensive team faces is a factor for calling offensive plays. In many instances, the offensive team has a greater play selection for 1st down and 2nd down, than they do for 3rd down. Which *down* an offensive team is on is certainly a factor for calling offensive plays.

Generally speaking, offensive teams are more at ease with *distance* when it's 10 yards or less to gain, with regards to securing a 1st down or a 1st & 10. For example, there are many offensive teams that are comfortable with a 1st down & 10 (1st down and 10 yards to go or gain), or (a 2nd down and 6 to go or gain), or a (3rd down and 2 yards to go or gain). Basically, offensive teams refer to these *downs* and *distances* as **manageable downs**, which simply means that their offensive team can run more sensible plays on these *downs* and *distances* without incurring too much risk. Most offensive teams do not like 3rd down situations with very long distances to go; for example, 3rd & 10, 3rd & 12, or 3rd & 15. The offensive team deems these situations to be both challenging and chancy. So, *distance* is indeed a factor for calling offensive plays.

Time is also a factor for calling offensive plays. When an offensive team is approaching halftime, they will call plays to preserve time on the game clock. When there's plenty of time of the game clock, they will run their regular plays, unless they are trailing by a large margin on the scoreboard.

Normally, offensive teams will stick to the script, or operate within the framework of their regular game plan, when the score is close or tied. The score throughout the course of the game is another factor for calling offensive plays. For this reason, some offensive teams will take a *conservative approach* when they have a two-touchdown lead or more. On the other hand, if the offensive team is down by two touchdowns or more, they will take a really *aggressive approach*.

Note: Some teams just simply do not match up well against certain teams. So, some offensive teams just do not match up well against certain defensive teams.

There are an excessive number of plays and type of plays that offensive teams run. Again, these selections of plays vary from team to team, as well as from coach to coach. I've created a category that I think all offensive plays fit into.

Offensive teams use 3 types of plays: Power plays, isolation plays, and setup plays. Of course, there are many variations of each type of play, but to simply things, think about these 3 types of plays when you watch an American football game.

1. Offensive teams use **power plays** when there is short distance or short yardage to go or gain (this means that the offensive team only needs to gain a small number of yards to secure a 1st down or 1st & 10). For example, the short yardage can be on a 3rd & short, a 4th & short, a 3rd & goal, or a 4th & goal (when the offensive team is on the goal line in scoring position).

   In many instances, you can recognize a *power play* because a team will run a play up the middle of the *offensive line* (OL) directly behind the center (C). And in other instances, they will run a *power play* behind the guards (LG, RG) or tackles (LT, RT). Usually, the offensive team will keep a *power play* on as much of a straight line as possible, in relation to the center of the offensive line (OL) in the running game, versus running the football outside of the tackles. They are staying cognizant of the fact that the quickest distance from one point to another is a straight line. Therefore, on a *power play*, an offensive team is going to run the football up the middle or as close to the middle of the offensive line as possible.

2. Offensive teams also use **isolation plays**. For example, when an offensive team has a star receiver, they may choose to run multiple plays for the receiver in order to isolate the opponents' defensive cornerback because they are sure they have an advantage. These *isolation plays* are great for key 1st downs and securing scoring opportunities. In most cases, *isolation plays* are designed with a particular star player in mind. The offensive team, as a result of studying the opposing defensive team's personnel and tendencies, know which areas of the defense, as well as which players, represent weakness.

3. Many offensive teams will routinely run a particular play or a play in a certain area of the field to set up another play. A **setup play** is when an offensive team runs a particular play for the sole purpose of setting up another play—generally, the follow-up play from the setup will yield greater results with regards to gaining territory and trying to score. This is one of the beauties of the nonstop chess match and in-depth strategies that go into an American football game. When *setup plays* leads to a successful follow-up play, it's always tremendously rewarding in these intense competitions. In American football, every sequence, down, and play has a winner and a loser. *Setup plays* are one more strategic way to try to win a play.

An offensive team having success in both the running game and passing game is the perfect formula for an offensive team. A *balanced attack* is when an offensive team has a balanced ratio of running plays to passing plays. In this instance, they can, in most cases, keep the defensive team off-balance. An offensive team normally has the advantage when they have a *balanced attack*—basically the defensive team has no idea what the offensive team is going to do next. Advantage: Offense. For example, when an offensive team has 60 offensive plays over the course of a game, and the coach calls 32 running plays and 28 passing plays, this is considered a *balanced attack*.

Looking at the game clock is something that all coaches and players do throughout the course of a game; they are looking at the amount of time remaining in any given quarter as well as at the score. There are four **quarters** in an American football game. Each **quarter** is called first quarter, second quarter, third quarter, and fourth quarter. The length of time for each quarter is the same, although the length of times for the quarters are different at the different levels—for middle-school football, high-school football, college football, and professional football. For example, in the NFL, each quarter is 15 minutes on the game clock.

Every football game is broken up into two halves, which are referred to as first half and second half. At the end of the first half, the teams go to intermission, which is referred to as **halftime**. After *halftime*, the second half begins.

Although a lot of focus is on the game clock, there's even more attention given to **managing the play clock**, in particular by the offensive team. The **play clock** indicates how much time an offensive team has to initiate or run their next play from the *line of scrimmage* without incurring a penalty. So, *managing the play clock* is something that's always on the minds of both a coach and a quarterback (QB) on every offensive play. The coach is responsible for calling the offensive plays from the sidelines in a timely fashion, and the quarterback is responsible for recalling that play in the huddle, getting up to the *line of scrimmage*, and then executing the play in time—thereby *managing the play clock*.

The offensive team is penalized when they do not run a play within the allotted time on the *play clock*. At the end of each offensive play, the referee blows the whistle and restarts the *play clock*. If you watch an American football game on television, quite often you will see the *play clock* displayed on the screen, especially when a quarterback (QB) comes close to not getting a play off before the *play clock* ticks down to zero.

Running or rushing the football is a major facet of American football for an offensive team. When the quarterback (QB) hands the football to a **running back** (RB) (the player who lines up behind the quarterback, receives the football by a handoff, and carries or runs the football to gain territory or score), this is referred to as a **running play**.

When an offensive team executes a *running play* or rushing play, whether it's an outside run, inside run, or a *power play*, etc., this is referred to as a phase of the game that's called the **running game**. All running plays constitute the *running game*.

In American football, most offensive teams want to have success in the *running game* for a number of reasons:

- One, when an offensive team has success in the *running game*, it can open up passing opportunities for *passing plays*. Again, this is part of the strategy for a *balanced attack*.
- Two, teams want to succeed in the *running game* because it's a safer mode of moving the football, attempting to gain territory, and attempting to score than passing the football, and many coaches feel like the risk of making a bad play is greater on *passing plays*.
- Three, a lot of teams want to succeed in the *running game* because of the *physical factor*. Most football teams want to be more physical than their opponents or win the physical battle because of the physical nature of the game. In general, most defensive teams are more physical than most offensive teams. So, when an offensive team dominates their opponents' defensive team with the *running game*, this means they are winning the physical battle.

Success in the *running game* is determined by the **average yards per carry/rush**, as well as the **total rushing yards** over the course of a game. For example, consider a team that has 60 plays over the course of a game, and they run 34 plays in the *running game* for an average of 4 yards per carry/rush. Because this offensive team had 34 plays in the *running game*, gaining territory of 4 yards on each run, they would finish the game with 136 *total rushing yards*. This is considered a great day in the *running game*. The milestone for the *running game* is 100 yards or as close to 100 yards as possible per game.

Passing or throwing the football is another major facet of American football for an offensive team. The quarterback (QB) passes or throws the football to a receiver (WR), tight end (TE), or running back (RB). When the offensive team executes a passing play or throws the football, this is referred to as the *passing game*.

When the quarterback (QB) passes or throws the football to a receiver and the intended receiver catches or completes the pass attempt by securing the football, it is called a **reception** or **completion**. When a receiver drops a pass attempt, or if the quarterback (QB) is inaccurate in his pass attempt and the receiver does not or is not able to complete the *reception*, it is referred to as an **incomplete pass**. The *reception of a pass* and the *incomplete pass* are more simply referred to as **complete** or **incomplete**, respectively.

Success in the *passing game*, in part, is determined by the ratio of *complete passes* to *incomplete passes*. For example, let's say the quarterback

(QB) attempts 25 passes over the course of a game and *completes* 20 of these pass attempts. (Note: The difference between *complete* passes and passes attempted represents the incomplete passes—20 of 25—which means there are 5 incomplete passes). This quarterback (QB) would be 20 of 25 in the *passing game*; this is considered a good game.

Another way success is determined in the *passing game* is by the total number of yards or *total passing yards* over the course of a game. Continuing with the same example, the quarterback (QB) *completes* 20 of 25 passes for a total of 250 passing yards; again, this is considered a good game.

Also, success in the *passing game* is determined by the quarterback's (QB) touchdown (TD) to **interception** (INT) ratio. This means, at the end of the game, how many touchdowns (TDs) did he throw, and how many *interceptions* did he throw? For example, the quarterback (QB) completes 20 of 25 passes, for 250 total passing yards, with 3 touchdowns (TDs) and 1 interception (INT). In this case, the touchdown (TD) to interception (INT) ratio is 3 to 1. Again, this would be a very successful passing game for an offensive team.

There are **Four Key Indicators for Success** for an offensive team: 3rd down conversions, turnover ratio, red zone success, and time of possession.

A **3rd down conversion** is when an offensive team is successful in gaining a total of 10 yards on 3rd down or the remaining balance of 10 yards on 3rd down. (For example, if the offensive team gained 3 yards on 1st down or their 1st attempt, then gained 2 yards on 2nd down or their 2nd attempt, and on 3rd down—their 3rd attempt—gained 5 yards, they gained the balance of the 10 yards needed to get a 1st down, or 1st & 10, on 3rd down, which means that they achieved a *3rd down conversion*).

When an offensive team gains 10 yards on 3rd down or the balance of the 10 yards needed from the 1st and 2nd down attempts by gaining the necessary yards needed for a 1st down on 3rd down (or their 3rd attempt), it is called a *3rd down conversion* because the result of the 1st down actually happened on their 3rd attempt or 3rd down. *3rd down conversions* are important because most teams will elect to punt on 4th down if they are not successful in getting a 1st down by their 3rd attempt/3rd down. The success an offensive team has on **3rd down conversions** is a good indicator for an offensive team's success in that particular game.

Every offensive team would like to prevail in the **turnover ratio**. Therefore, it's important to protect or hold onto the football while executing an offensive play and not commit a *turnover* (this is when the team that has possession of the football loses or gives up possession of the football to

Reginald "Reggie" Jones

the opponent by either a fumble or an *interception*). Note: A fumble is when a player has possession of the football and accidently drops or loses control of the football or has the football taken away or knocked away from his possession by a defensive player.

The *turnover ratio* is the total number of times a team *turns over* the football compared to the total number of times their opponents *turn over* the football throughout the game. For example, the home team finishes the game with 2 *turnovers*, and the visiting team finishes the game with 4 *turnovers*. The home team would win the *turnover ratio*, 4 to 2. *Turnovers* are almost always significant in wins and losses in American football—it's an anomaly when the reverse happens. A football team loses the *turnover ratio* significantly, yet still wins the game—it's rare but can certainly happen.

Red zone success is another major indicator for an offensive team's success. The *red zone* is the area of the football field when an offensive team is 20 yards or less from their opponents' *end zone* (the end zone they are trying to get to in order to score a touchdown). It's very important for an offensive team to have *red zone success*, because it's routinely a challenge to get into this area of the field. And it's important for an offensive team to capitalize on *red zone success* because they are in such close striking distance to the end zone. Almost all offensive teams highlight the necessity to have *red zone success*.

Time of possession is another key indicator of an offensive team's success. *Time of possession* is exactly what is says—it's the total amount of time an offensive team possesses or has the football in their hands over the course of a game. The reason teams want to win the *time of possession* battle is because the more time their offensive team is on the football field with possession of the football, the more opportunities they will have to attempt to score. In addition, the more time their own offensive team is on the field with possession of the football means more time that their opponents' offensive team is spending on the bench, with fewer opportunities to attempt to score. Most offensive teams place an enormous amount of emphasis on winning the *time of possession* battle.

The play and performance of the offensive team is at its best when they are successful on *3rd down conversions*. By having success on 3rd down conversions, the offensive team helps their defensive team get more rest on the bench. Note: The offensive team gets a new set of 4 downs (or 4 attempts) every time they are successful on a *3rd down conversion*; therefore, the offensive team continues to try to gain territory or score, while their defensive team continues to rest.

The play and performance of the offensive team is at its best when it complements their defensive team by winning the *turnover ratio*. When an offensive team wins the *turnover ratio*, they help their defensive team by not putting them in bad field position as a result of a *turnover*. In many instances, a turnover will leave the defensive team in a precarious position. When an offensive team avoids turnovers and punts the football on 4th down, they play strategically—by putting the opponents' offensive team in bad field position.

The play and performance of the offensive team is at its best when it complements their defensive team by having *red zone success*. When an offensive team has *red zone success*, they help their defensive team by putting points up on the scoreboard. Every time an offensive team puts points on the scoreboard, they create a greater points margin for their opponents' offensive team to have to overcome. The offensive team is helping their defensive team by having a greater margin of points to defend against the opponents' offensive team. In most instances, this allows the defensive team to be more aggressive.

The play and performance of the offensive team is at its best when it complements their defensive team by winning the *time of possession* battle. When an offensive team wins the *time of possession* battle, they help their defensive team by allowing them to stay off the field and get more rest for the next series. Also, the more time the *offensive team* is on the football field with possession of the football, the more opportunities they will have to attempt to score.

Again, the more time the offensive team is on the field with possession of the football is also time that their opponents' offensive team is spending on the bench. So the offensive team is complementing their defensive team by neutralizing the opponents' offensive team by winning the *time of possession* battle.

Indeed, the offensive team is expected to be the *point producers*, by generating enough points to win the game. Nevertheless, you are watching football at its best when one unit compliments another unit. The success of the offensive team certainly complements the success of the defensive team.

CHAPTER 3

Defensive Team

"Alpha-male"

The **defensive team** is expected to be the **score stoppers**. The scheme or system that most *defensive teams* use to stop their opponents' offensive team from scoring points is different in most cases, and it varies greatly from team to team, as well as from coach to coach. The plan of attack that most *defensive teams* use to compete against their opponents' offensive team usually contrasts greatly from the plan of attack used by offensive teams.

Remember, while most *offensive teams* take on more of a finesse attitude, most *defensive teams* take on more of a physical posture, which means that most of what they design and do is centered on being more physical than their opponents' offensive team. Most defensive players are more of the **alpha-male** types. While the offensive team will typically try to outsmart the opponents' defensive team, most defensive teams will try to be more physical and more aggressive than the opponents' offensive team, while at the same time placing an emphasis on playing smart football.

Once more, in American football, there are 11 players from each team on the football field all of the time. When one defensive team is on the field with their 11 defensive players, the opponents' offensive team is on the field with their 11 offensive players. It's always 11 against 11.

Now it's time to meet the 11 players who represent the **defensive team**:

The role of the **defensive linemen** (DL) is to tackle the opponents' running backs (RBs) on running plays and try to restrict their ability to gain territory or score. *Defensive linemen* (DL) also attempt to attack or put pressure on the opponents' quarterback (QB) on passing plays, and if possible, **sack** the quarterback (QB). (To *sack* the quarterback means to tackle the quarterback on a passing play behind the line of scrimmage, thereby forcing the opposing team to lose yards.) *Defensive linemen* are the first line of defense. The *Defensive linemen's* (DL) position coach is called the **defensive line coach**.

Individual **defensive line** positions include:

- Nose guard (NG)
- Left defensive tackle (LDT)
- Left defensive end (LDE)
- Right defensive tackle (RDT)
- Right defensive end (RDE).

The **nose guard** (NG) is especially counted on to be a **run stopper**—to tackle the opponents' running backs (RBs) on running plays; generally, the *nose guard* is really tough on running plays. This player, in many instances, lines up in front of the offensive team's center (C); however, on occasions, he may line up on the left or right of the center (C). The *nose guard's* (NG) position coach is called the **defensive line coach** or **D-Line coach**.

The **defensive tackles** (DTs—LDT and RDT) are always lined up on each side of the nose guard. Their role is to be **run stoppers** as well. They are also expected to put pressure on the opponents' quarterback (QB) on passing plays. The *defensive tackles'* (DT) position coach is called the *defensive linemen coach* or *D-Line coach*.

The **defensive ends** (DEs: LDE and RDE) are expected to stop the offensive team from gaining territory to the outside of the defensive alignment on running plays and to stop the opponents' running backs (RBs) from running the football on the sidelines. The *defensive ends* (DEs) are also expected to put pressure on the opponents' quarterback, knock down the opponents' pass attempts, or *sack* the quarterback (QB) on passing plays. (Note: You will often hear sports announcers refer to **set the edge** or **setting the edge**. This terminology is used often in reference to the defensive ends' responsibility to maintain outside containment; it means that it's the defensive ends' job to not let any running back run outside of him or get around him.) *Defensive ends'* (DEs) position coach is called the *defensive linemen coach* or *D-Line coach*.

There are typically three or four *defensive linemen* on the field; again, the *nose guard*, in many instances, lines up in front of the offensive team's center (C). The *left defensive tackle* (LDT) lines up to the left of the nose guard; the *left defensive end* (LDE) lines up to the left of the left defensive tackle (LDT). The *right defensive tackle* (RDT) lines up to the right of the nose guard; the *right defensive end* (RDE) lines up to the right of the right defensive tackle.

The **linebackers** (LBs) are the players who get a lot of action and make a lot of tackles. There is a **middle linebacker** (MLB) and **outside linebackers** (OLBs). The type of defense a defensive team uses determines how many *linebackers* are used. The *linebackers'* job is to back up the defensive linemen, to stop the opponents' running backs (RBs) on running plays, and to assist with coverage on passing plays. Oftentimes, the *linebackers* (LBs) have a clear path to hit the running backs (RBs) because of the job their defensive linemen do in taking on blockers (offensive linemen). As a result, the linebackers (LBs), in most cases, will get a large number of the tackles for a defensive team. *Outside linebackers* line up on the left side and the right side of the *middle linebacker*. The *linebackers* are the second line of defense. The *linebackers'* (LB) position coach is called the **linebackers coach**. Often, the *linebackers coach* is the most intense coach on the defensive team. Although sometimes it's hard to tell; most of the defensive team position coaches tend to be more intense than the offensive team position coaches.

Note: If a defensive team uses 3 defensive linemen and 4 linebackers, this team is playing what's called a **3-4 defense**. Conversely, if a defensive team uses 4 defensive lineman and 3 linebackers, this team is playing what's called a **4-3 defense**; these are the two most commonly used defenses in the NFL (National Football League).

The **cornerbacks'** (CBs) role is primarily as pass-defenders. The *cornerbacks'* (CBs) responsibility is to prevent the wide receivers (WRs) from catching the football; they do this by breaking up intended passes to receivers and by intercepting passes from the quarterback when possible. (Remember that *intercepting* is when the defensive player creates a *turnover* by catching a pass from the opponents' quarterback that was intended for a receiver.) In addition, the *cornerback* has a responsibility on running plays to stop the running back from getting outside of the defense and to stop him from scoring.

The *cornerback* position, naturally, is my favorite position on the field since this is the position I played. Aside from the quarterback position, I believe the *defensive cornerback* (CB) position is the most difficult position to play in American football. Quite often the phrase **being on an island** or **on the island alone** is used with regards to the *cornerback* (CB) because he is left all alone to defend a receiver deep down the field. A player cannot play the *cornerback* (CB) position with any level of efficiency if he does not "**drop-a-set**" (a full explanation of this phrase can be found in chapter 7— it's often associated with being bold and brave in the football vernacular).

A football player cannot play the cornerback position if he has courage the size of a G-string.

The *cornerback* (CB) position necessitates having the skill to run backwards; it's also necessary to have the most-flexible hips for the agile movements required to keep up with the many moves of the receivers, and it's essential to have great footwork. Generally speaking, the *defensive backs* (DBs)—which includes the *cornerbacks*—are the very best, fastest, and most highly skilled athletes on the defensive team. There is a **left cornerback** (LCB) and a **right cornerback** (RCB). The cornerback position is part of the last line of defense as it pertains to stopping the offense from gaining territory or scoring. The *cornerbacks'* (CB) position coach is called the **defensive backs coach** or the **DB coach**. Note: When a defensive team encounters an obvious passing scenario because of *down* and *distance* or the extra number of *receivers* in the game, they will use five *defensive backs* (called a "**nickel defense**" or "**nickel package**") or six *defensive backs* (called a "**dime defense**" or "**dime package**"). Usually in both the *nickel package* and *dime package*, the extra *defensive backs* are backup *cornerbacks*.

Safeties (S) generally line up deep behind the rest of the defense in order to prevent long running plays and long passing plays. There are two *safeties*: a **strong safety** (SS) and a **free safety** (FS). The *strong safety* usually lines up on the side of the field where there are more offensive players (this side is referred to as the **strong side** of the offensive team). The *strong safety* is usually involved in more running plays than the *free safety* but also still has passing responsibilities as a *defensive back* (DB). In some cases, the *strong safety* (SS) is so big, strong, and fast that he is like a super-talented linebacker because of his ability to be extremely physical and do major damage to the offensive team on running plays. As a result, the *strong safety*, in many cases, will record more tackles than the *free safety*. The *strong safety* (SS) position coach is called the *defensive backs coach* or the *DB coach*.

The **free safety** plays a deep middle position on the field in many instances, though on some passing plays, the *free safety* (FS) and the strong safety (SS) share equal responsibility in the coverage of half of the field in pass coverage. The *free safety*, the strong safety (SS), and cornerbacks (CBs) are the line of defense on running plays and passing plays. The *free safety*, in many instances, will get the most interceptions for a defensive team since his primary role is to defend the pass and not let any receivers (WRs) get behind him. Also, because he does not have primary run responsibilities and he's always watching the quarterback (QB), the *free safety* (FS) is often in a position to make a play on most passing plays. The *free safety* (FS) position coach is called the *defensive backs coach* or the *DB coach*.

Notice, you will often hear a sports announcer say that a defensive player made a tackle *in space* or make a reference to action taking place *in space*. This phrase refers to the open field (this is generally the area of the football field away from all of the other players, where, in most cases, a defensive player is one-on-one against an offensive player). In theory, the offensive player should have an advantage because of the open field or open space.

When a team does not have possession of the football, it is on defense. The defensive team uses a number of methods to prevent the opponents' offensive team from gaining territory and scoring. The defensive team does this by knocking down, pushing down, grabbing, flipping, wrapping up, or tackling an opposing offensive player. This is all a part of the physical nature of the game but especially the physical nature of a defensive team.

There are 3 levels (3 lines of the defense) of a defensive team that an offensive team has to penetrate in order to score a *touchdown*. (Note: An offensive team can gain territory by penetrating either of the first 2 levels of a defensive team; however, in most cases, an offensive team has to penetrate all 3 levels of a defensive team in order to score a touchdown. The exception in this case is on the goal line.)

Lines of Defense:
- The 1st line of defense—defensive linemen
- 2nd line of defense—linebackers
- 3rd line of defense—defensive backs

The defensive team also uses **situational preparation** (planning and preparing for different situations by studying the opponents' personnel and tendencies) to prepare for the opponents' offensive team. Typically, the defensive team also prepares from two perspectives; the first is based on the defensive team's own philosophy, strength, and game plan. The second is based on what the opposing offensive team's strengths and weaknesses are, as well as whether the opposing offensive team takes a conservative approach or an aggressive approach. This *situational preparation* is done in the form of studying and reviewing the opponents' tendencies (what type of plays they prefer, when they like to run the plays, and where on the field and how often they like to run the plays). In *situational* *preparation*, the defensive team tries to prepare for every possible situation and scenario they may encounter against the opponents' offensive team.

And the same is true for the players on the defensive team as it was for the players on the offensive team—the team player always takes situational preparation seriously, with a concentrated focus and intense attention to details. He is very much unlike the selfish player who has a fickle focus and is often detached when it comes to attention to details. Again, the selfish player is on and off with regards to preparation because he takes his opponent and preparation lightly.

The **defensive game plan** is the segment of the coaches' overall game plan, specifically designed as a **plan of attack** for the defensive team against the opponents' offensive team. The *defensive game plan* is usually designed with a strategy for stopping the opponents' offensive team in their running game and passing game. This strategy is structured in the form of a **run defense** and a **pass defense**.

One coach will choose a conservative approach with their run defense and an aggressive approach with their pass defense, while another coach may have a defensive game plan that calls for an aggressive approach in the run defense and a conservative approach in the pass defense. Then, there's another coach who has a defensive game plan where he chooses an **aggressive attack**, choosing to aggressively attack the opponents' offensive team with an aggressive approach in both the run defense and the pass defense, equally. The strategy in this case is to try to dominate with the defensive team.

Some defensive teams have a coach who will take a conservative approach or aggressive approach based on the field position that an offensive team has, meaning that if the offensive team has really bad field position, the coach will take an aggressive approach. Conversely, if the offensive team has great field position, the coach will take a conservative approach.

An interesting footnote: Sometimes an offensive team's or defensive team's reason for taking a conservative approach, especially when they don't normally take such an approach, is simply a **confidence shortage** (they have no confidence in taking any risks against a very challenging opponent).

More often than not, the *alpha-male types* of the defensive team have the mindset that if you have an opponent down, not only do you put your foot on their throat but you also dig it into their throat and bury them. Whereas, offensive teams, with their finesse attitude, typically have the mindset of preserving their lead when their opponents are down.

The intensity of a defensive team is always high because most defensive players feel like they are tougher than their offensive competitors. And most defensive players are intent on displaying that aggressive attitude every time they play a game. In the NFL, there are a lot of defensive players who play with a chip on their shoulders because they feel like the league is an offense-driven league (scoring is vital for entertainment value and fan satisfaction). There some defensive players in the NFL who feel like a lot of the rules favor the offensive players and the offensive teams. This group of players and the alpha-male types are responsible for the intensity of a defensive team.

Most defensive players do not want to see an offensive player seriously injured. I'm certainly not a fan of it and do not endorse it—especially since injuries ended my own NFL career. However, when it comes to inflicting temporary pain and causing an offensive player to have his *manhood minimized*—ABSOLUTELY!!!

There are typically 4 **factors for calling defensive plays**: *Field position, down and distance, time,* and *score.*

Most defensive teams are flexible as it relates to sticking to the script and calling their defensive plays throughout the course of a game. Nevertheless, **field position** is a factor for calling defensive plays. Some defensive teams will take a really conservative approach or a really aggressive approach, based on the *field position* of an offensive team. If the offensive team has really bad *field position*, the coach will take a really *aggressive approach* as far as calling defensive plays. On the other hand, if the offensive team has great *field position*, the coach will take a really conservative approach as far as calling defensive plays.

Down and **distance** are also factors for calling defensive plays. Defensive teams want to force the opponents' offensive team into late downs and long distance situations—for example, 3 & 10, 3 & 15, 4 & 10, and 4 & 15. Defensive teams strive to win on 1st down against the opponents' offensive team in order to try to get an advantage for the series. All defensive teams know that the offensive team does not want to be in 3rd & long situations, so it's important for the defensive team to win on 1st down, maintain on 2nd down and force the opponents' offensive team into 3rd & long (3rd & 10, 3rd & 12, 3rd & 15, etc.) In American football, every sequence, down, and play has a winner and a loser. So, the offensive team has a similar aim—to win on 1st down in an effort to create an advantage and have *manageable downs.* (Note: When the offensive team has a large gain in territory on 1st down, leaving a small amount of yards remaining for 2nd and 3rd downs, it is considered a "manageable down.") Defensive teams have a far greater advantage on 3rd & long situations.

Likewise, **time** is a factor for calling defensive plays. If a defensive team is winning the game and there is a limited amount of *time* on the game clock for their opponents' offensive team to make a comeback, the defensive team will take a really conservative approach. In the opposite situation, if the defensive team is losing the game, and there is a limited amount of *time* on the game clock for their own offensive team to make a comeback, the defensive team will take a really aggressive approach to try to get the football back so their offensive team can attempt to score.

Furthermore, the **score** is a factor for calling defensive plays. If a defensive team falls behind by two scores or more, generally the defensive team will call more aggressive defensive plays. On the other hand, if a defensive team is up by two scores or more, in many instances, the defensive team will become more conservative as it relates to calling defensive plays. Typically, when the score is tied or close, most defensive teams will execute their normal game plan without any major adjustments. Note: There are a lot of offensive teams that will narrow their play selection in really tight games.

Remember that some teams just simply do not match up well against certain teams. So, the fact of the matter is that some defensive teams just do not match up well against certain offensive teams.

Most defensive teams, as a strategy, would like to make their opponents' offensive team **one-dimensional**. This is a dominating stage of the game. When a defensive team is at the stage of the game where they make their opponents' offensive team *one-dimensional*, it means that the defensive team has shut down, or totally stopped and made non-existent, either the opposing offensive team's *running game* or *passing game*.

In many instances, the defensive team will make the opposing offensive team *one-dimensional* in the *running game* by simply getting great penetration at the line of scrimmage from the defensive line (DL) and by the defensive line (DL) making tackles at the line of scrimmage on the running plays. When the defensive line (DL) is penetrating and making tackles at the line of scrimmage, they also create a clear path for their linebackers (LBs) to come in and totally clean up on running plays.

Another way a defensive team dominates the opponent in the running game is by doing what defensive teams call putting **8-in-the-box**. This means that the defensive team is committing all of their defensive linemen (DLs), all of their linebackers (LBs), and their strong safety (SS) to their *run defense* and taking the risk to leave their two cornerbacks (CBs) and free safety (FS) in one-on-one man coverage, with no help in their *pass defense*. This strategy is used when the defensive team is determined to shut down the opponents' running game.

When the defensive team makes the opponents' offensive team one-dimensional in the running game, it forces the opponents to focus primarily on their passing game. Because the defensive team is aware of the fact that they are dominating in this phase and at this stage of the game, they are even more prepared and ready to defend the opponents' passing game. This situation creates some extremely challenging conditions for an offensive team.

There are other instances when the defensive team will make the opponents' offensive team one-dimensional by taking away or shutting down their passing game. The defensive team does this in one of two ways, or both at the same time. One way a defensive team makes the opponents' offensive team one-dimensional is by implementing a great **pass rush**, which is when they are constantly putting pressure on the opponents' quarterback (QB), disrupting (causing the quarterback to rush and make errors), knocking down passes, and sacking the quarterback (QB) on passing plays. (Remember that *sacking the quarterback* means tackling him behind the line of scrimmage, thereby forcing the opponents to lose yards, on passing plays.) The other way, a defensive team can make the opponents' offensive team one-dimensional is by having great **pass coverage** by the defensive backs, not allowing the opponents' receivers (WRs) to catch any or very many *completions*, especially any that yield a significant gain in territory or a score.

Note: There are times when the defensive team's *pass rush* complements the *pass coverage*, meaning, the pass rush is so good, it forces the quarterback (QB) to throw a bad pass or run with the football. Similarly, there are times when the defensive team's pass coverage is so good that the defensive backs (DBs) do not allow any of the receivers (WRs) to get open for the quarterback (QB) to throw the football to; this situation forces the quarterback (QB) to hold the football longer than he should, ultimately resulting in a sack. This is commonly referred to as a **coverage sack** (when the *pass coverage* of the defensive backs creates more time for a lineman or linebacker to secure a sack).

When the defensive team makes the opponents' offensive team one-dimensional in the passing game, it forces the opponents' offensive team to focus primarily on their running game. Again, because the defensive team is aware of the fact that they are dominating in this phase and at this stage of the game, they are even more prepared and ready to defend the opponents' running game, and this creates some extremely challenging conditions for the offensive team.

The livelihood of a good defensive team is when they make their opponents' offensive team one-dimensional. For a defensive team, this is the most dominating stage of the game; the defensive team is not only controlling the rhythm and pace for the offensive team, they are actually impacting offensive-play-calling as well. The defensive team is now dictating what the opponents' offensive team can and cannot do.

When I played with the New Orleans Saints, I was fortunate to play with a number of great defensive players; one in particular was a great run stopper and a great pass rusher who also played with great intensity. It was an honor to play with Pro Football Hall of Famer Rickey Jackson—linebacker.

Because the running game is a major facet of American football for an offensive team, the *run defense* is a major facet of American football for a defensive team. When the defensive team executes plays against the running game of the opponents' offensive team, it is called the **run defense**.

In American football, most defensive teams want to dominate their opponents' offensive team with the *run defense* for different reasons. First, the defensive team knows that if the opponents' offensive team has a lot of success in the running game against their defensive team, it can open up passing opportunities for their opponents in the passing game. The defensive team is aware of the fact that it's a strategy of the opponents' offensive team to have a balanced attack. Second, the defensive team also knows that the opponents' offensive team would like to succeed in the running game because they feel like it's a safer mode of moving the football in an attempt to gain territory and score than passing the football. Finally, the defensive team knows that a lot of offensive teams want to succeed in the running game because of the physical factor. Most football teams want to be more physical than their opponents, or win the physical battle, simply because of the physical nature of the game. Of course, most defensive teams believe they are more physical than their opponents' offensive teams.

For a good run defense, a defensive team counts on penetration from their defensive linemen (DL), as well as **sure tackling** (meaning no missed tackles) from their entire defensive team. Most defensive linemen (DLs) and linebackers (LBs) are proud to be **run stoppers** (defensive players who routinely stop or stuff the opponents' running plays—for defensive linemen, it's called **winning in the trenches**; this catchphrase is in reference to the area where the offensive linemen and defensive linemen battle it out at the line of scrimmage). The defensive teams that have *run stoppers* are also efficient in their **short yardage defense** (the defense designed to stop the opponents when they are in a 3rd & 2, 3rd & 1, or 4th & 1, or 4th & inches scenario) and **goal-line defense** (when the opponents' offensive team is on the goal line in position to score a touchdown). Most defensive teams embrace the physicality that comes with having a good *run defense*.

Because the passing game is a major facet of American football for an offensive team, the **pass defense** is a major facet of American football for a defensive team. When the defensive team executes plays against the passing game of the opponents' offensive team, it is called the *pass defense*.

Defensive teams recognize the fact that, by running isolation plays and setup plays in their passing game, the opponents' offensive team would like to have success against their pass defense. So, the defensive team is prepared the support their defensive backs (DBs) when the opponents' offensive team tries to isolate the star receiver (WR) against their defensive backs (DBs). Also, defensive teams rely on disciplined execution from the defensive backs (DBs) and linebackers (LBs) when it comes to their opponents' offensive team running setup plays in their passing game. The defensive team knows that the most common *setup play* in the passing game for an offensive team is called **play action pass**. This is when the offensive team runs the football up the middle of the offensive line over and over, several times; then the offensive team will come back and fake the same running play they ran over and over, but they will actually throw a passing play. In many instances, this fake running play or *play action pass*, will sometimes draw the safeties (S) in for the run fake, and in many cases will draw in the linebackers (LBs), and it will open up the offensive team's receivers (WRs) so they can complete a pass.

Not only do defensive teams try to apply pass pressure to the quarterback (QB), they also try to limit his completion by knocking down attempted passes. Defensive teams know that most offensive teams want their offensive team (quarterback) to have a 65% to 70% **completion rate** (the percent of passes completed compared to the number of passes attempted or incomplete passes).

Remember the example of the quarterback (QB) in chapter 2 with the good passing game? The quarterback was 20 of 25: 20 pass completions in 25 passes attempted for 250 passing yards, with 3 touchdowns (TDs) and 1 interception (INT). In this example, the quarterback (QB) would have an 80% *completion rate*. This would not be a good day for the defensive team in their pass defense. So, defensive teams try vigorously to stop the quarterback (QB) and offensive team from having success against their pass defense. A good *pass defense* generally will have a good balance of pass rush and pass coverage.

There are **3 Key Indicators for Success for a Defensive Team**.

- When a defensive team gets a **3-and-out** (when the defensive team holds the offensive team to 3 unsuccessful attempts at securing a 1st down or 1st & 10, and as a result, the offensive team elects to punt the football on 4th down), it is a key indicator for success for a defensive team. The defensive team is aware of the fact that offensive teams want to be successful in their *3rd down conversions*. Defensive teams always stress getting off the field on 3rd downs. The situation *3-and-out* is always: Advantage—defense. When a defensive team is successful in getting consecutive *3-and-outs*, they put a lot of pressure on the opponents' offensive team, and they give their own offensive team more opportunities to attempt to score. The *3-and-out* is a key indicator for success for a defensive team.

- Winning the **turnover ratio** is another key indicator for success for a defensive team. Again, both the defensive team and their opponents' offensive team would like to win the turnover ratio or turnover battle. (Remember that a *turnover* is when a team loses possession of the football to the opponents, by either fumble or interception.) As in most cases, the team that wins the turnover ratio wins the game. In most instances, turnovers and a negative turnover ratio have an adverse effect on the outcome of the game in American football. So, *turnover ratio* is a key indicator for success for a defensive team.

- The *red zone defense* is a key indicator for success for a defensive team. Remember, the red zone is the area of the football field where the opponents' offensive team is 20 yards or less away from the end zone. The defensive team recognizes how important it is for their opponents' offensive team to score a touchdown (TD) once they get into the red zone. It's a major challenge for the opponents' offensive team to get into the red zone frequently. Consequently, the defensive team plays with the highest level of intensity and with supreme focus in their *red zone defense* in order to hold their opponents' offensive team to *field goals* (3 points versus the 6 points for a *touchdown*). *Red zone defense* is absolutely a key indicator for success for a defensive team.

The play and performance of the defensive team is at its best when it complements their offensive team by having success with a *3-and-out*. When a defensive team has a successful or consecutive 3-and-out, they help their offensive team by putting them back on the football field, thereby giving them another opportunity to score and additional opportunities to win the time of possession battle over their opponent. By having success with 3-and-outs, the defensive team diminishes the opponents' offensive team's ability to have success with their 3rd down conversions, diminishing the opposing offensive team's ability to gain territory and score.

The play and performance of the defensive team is at its best when it complements their offensive team by winning the *turnover ratio*. When a defensive team wins the turnover ratio, they help their offensive team by giving them possession of the football again. Remember, every time the offensive team gets possession of the football, it gives them another opportunity to score, and it adds to their time of possession total. In many instances, a turnover will put the team who secured the turnover in good field position.

The play and performance of the defensive team is at its best when it complements their offensive team by having success with their *red zone defense*. When a defensive team has success with their red zone defense, they help their offensive team by reducing the amount of points the opposing offensive team puts up on the scoreboard, thereby creating a smaller points margin for their own offensive team to score in order for them to help win the game. Every time a defensive team, as a result of their red zone defense, limits the number of points their opponents' offensive team puts on the scoreboard, they create a greater challenge for their opponents' offensive team to overcome since the number of times that an offensive team gets to the red zone are usually limited.

Indeed, the defensive team members are expected to be the *score stoppers* by holding the opponents' offensive team to fewer points than their own offensive team puts up on the scoreboard. Without a doubt, you experience American football at its best when one unit complements another unit. The success of the defensive team positively complements the success of the offensive team.

CHAPTER 4

Special Teams

Aesthetics

*T*he **special teams** is expected to be a **field position creator** and **point creator**. Like the offensive teams and defensive teams, the scheme or system that most *special teams* use to stop their opponents' *special teams* from gaining field position and scoring points varies greatly from team to team as well as from coach to coach.

Most special teams take on an aggressive approach, and their players are similar to defensive players, in that many of them passionately embrace the physicality of the game. In fact, many of the special teams players totally sacrifice their bodies on multiple special teams plays.

Once more: In American football, there are 11 players from each team on the football field all of the time. When the special teams is on the field with its 11 special teams' players, the opponents' special teams is on the field with its 11 special teams' players. The game is always 11 against 11.

Let's meet the 11 different players and types of positions that represent the special teams:

The **kicker** or **placekicker** (K) is the special teams' player who kicks the football from a tee, at the beginning of an American football game and at the beginning of the second half; he also kicks the football after every successful field goal and touchdown (specifically after the extra-point attempt or two-point-conversion attempt following a touchdown). Usually, the *kicker* does the kicking for the extra-point attempt and field-goal attempt. (There are exceptions where a team will have a *kicker* for kick-offs and a different *kicker* for extra points and field goals.) Note: A *kicker* does not use a tee when kicking an extra point or field goal. In these two instances, the football is received by a **holder** and placed on the field for the *kicker* to attempt either the extra point or the field goal, respectively.

The kicker, in many instances, is one of the players on the team who falls into the *fragile confidence* group. Often, if the kicker misses consecutive field goals in a game or in consecutive games, he may have to deal with his own *fragile confidence*. In most cases, kickers are role players, but, occasionally, a kicker is a star player.

The **punter** (P) is the special teams' player who kicks the football, usually on 4th down in American football. Notice, the direction of the football and/or the direction the team is moving changes when there is a change of possession, but the punter **punts**/kicks the football in the same direction the offensive is going. The direction an offensive team is going also changes at the end of the 1st quarter, after halftime and the end of the 3rd quarter.

The punter is generally called into action after the offensive team has failed to get or secure a 1st down (1st & 10). Remember, this is done by gaining a total of 10 yards. Most teams will try to accomplish this on their first 3 downs of the 4 downs allowed (meaning on the 1st down/1st attempt, 2nd down/2nd attempt, and 3rd down/3rd attempt), and if they are not successful in gaining the 10 yards necessary for a 1st down, in most cases, the offensive team will elect to *punt* the football on 4th down (the 4th attempt allowed to get a 1st down). Also, the *punter* receives the football directly from the **long snapper** before he executes the *punt* (kick). Generally, *punters* are role players.

Note: The *punter*, unlike the kicker, *receives* (or catches) the football in order to kick it. The kicker does not directly receive the football from the snapper. Again, the kicker uses a *tee* for the kickoff, and the kicker has a *holder* for extra-point and field-goal attempts.

In most cases, when the *punter* kicks the football, he focuses on **hang time** (when the punter specifically tries to kick the football as high and as far as possible) in order to allow the coverage men/tacklers enough time to run down the football field and make a tackle on the opponents' **punt-returner** (the special teams' player who catches/returns the punt). The *punter* also has to have the skills to do what's called a **directional punt** (when the punt team is challenged with a great *punt-returner* and they would like to try to box him in on the sidelines, the punter can kick the football on either side of the field.) Also, a *directional punt* is used strategically when a punt team wants to win the field position battle; the punter will attempt to kick the football out of bounds inside of the 10-yard line, creating bad field position for the opponents' offensive team.

After the *punter* has kicked (*punted*) the football and the opponents' punt-returner has *returned* the football, you will often hear the sports announcer on television make a reference to **net kick** of 40, 45, 50 yards, etc. For example, let's say the *punter* kicks (*punts*) the football and it travels from the line of scrimmage 60 yards to the spot (line on the football field) where the *punt-returner* catches the football. Then the punt-returner *returns* (runs with) the football for 15 yards (gaining territory of 15 yards). The *net kick* is the total distance or yards the football was initially kicked (punted), less the return yards. In this example, the *punt* was for 60 yards and the *return* was for 15 yards, so the punter would have a *net kick* of 45 yards.

The **punt-returner** or **punt-return man** (PR) is the special teams' player whose role is twofold; the first is to *catch* (secure possession of) the football that's kicked (referred to as *punted*) by the opponents' punter. The second is to *return* (run with) the football for as many yards as possible (*gain territory*) in order to put his offensive team in the best field position possible.

Note: When the punt-returner thinks that returning the football is too risky, meaning that the opponents' punter has kicked (punted) the football successfully with a lot of *hang time*, and the punt-returner will not be able to catch and return the football before the coverage men/tacklers approach him, the punt-returner can execute what's called a **fair catch**; a *fair catch* is when the punt-returner signals that he is electing to catch the football without having the option to return or advance the football, and in this situation, the coverage men/tacklers are not permitted to touch or hit the punt-returner. The punt-returner executes a *fair catch* by waving one hand high in the air across his face and head, for the coverage men and officials to see. When a *fair catch* (safe catch) is executed, the offensive team will get possession of the football at the spot (line on the football field) where the punt-returner made the fair catch. In most cases, when the punt-returner executes a *fair catch* (safe catch), he is taking a cautious approach to securing possession of the football for the offensive team. The punt-returner is generally motivated to make a decision for a fair catch by how close the coverage men are to him as he is about to receive the kick (punt). In order to avoid taking a big hit and/or losing possession of the football, the punt-returner will execute the fair catch.

Also, the punt-returner, as a general rule, is coached not to return a punt that is inside of the 10-yard line because this creates really bad field position for the offensive team; therefore, the punt-returner will attempt to allow the football to go into the end zone for what's called a **touchback** (when the opponents' punt team kicks the football into the end zone and the punt-returner allows it to go into the end zone without a return attempt so their offensive team will be allowed to get the football and start their next drive or series on the 20-yard line). In some instances, the punt-returner is a star player; however, in most cases, the punt-returner is a role player.

The **kickoff-returner** or **kickoff-return man** (KR) is another special teams' player whose role is twofold; the first is to *catch* (secure possession of) the football that's kicked by the opponents' kicker (from the opponents' kickoff team). The second is to *return* (run with) the football for as many yards as possible (*gain territory*) in order to put his offensive team in the best field position possible. In some instances, a kickoff-returner is a star player; however, in most cases, the kickoff returner is a role player.

The **long snapper** or **snapper** (LS) is the special teams' player whose role is to *snap* the football as fast and as accurately as possible. (*To snap the football* in this case means to pass it from the same position as the offensive center and initiate certain special teams plays.) This specialty *snapper* is referred to as a *long snapper* because, unlike the center on the offensive team who in most cases snaps the football directly into the hands of the quarterback, the *long snapper* will snap the football over a greater distance. For example, the long snapper snaps the football to the holder over a range of 6 to 8 yards on extra-point attempts, and he snaps the football to the holder over a range of 12 to 15 yards on field-goal attempts. The long snapper is always a role player.

The **holder** (H) is the special teams' player who catches the football from the long snapper, places the football on the field, and holds it steady (many holders use either one or two fingers to hold the football). Note: The holder will always rotate the football to ensure that the kicker does not kick the white laces (the term **laces out** means that the laces should be facing out, away from the kicker—specifically toward the goal posts). The reason kickers do not like to kick the white laces is because they don't have control of the kick when they kick the white laces. Therefore, securing, placing, and rotating the laces on the football are important aspects of good execution for the *holder*. The *holder* holds the football for the kicker on both extra points and field goals. The holder is always a role player, though quite often is also the backup quarterback (QB).

Blockers (Bs) are the special teams' players who are responsible for **blocking** (guarding and stopping) the opponents' rushers on different phases of the special teams—whether it's blocking during an extra-point attempt, field-goal attempt, or punt. The *blockers* are generally role players.

Coverage men are the special teams' players who are responsible for running down the field and tackling, knocking down to the ground, or knocking out of bounds the returner (punt-returner and kickoff-returner). The *coverage men* are generally role players.

Note: The coverage men on the kickoff team, before and after the kickoff, are coverage men, which means that when these players line up for the *kickoff*, they are *coverage men*, and when they run down the football field with the sole intent to tackle, knock down to the ground, or knock out of bounds the kick-returner, they are still *coverage men/tacklers*.

However, note that when *coverage men* line up on the punt team, the end game may be to tackle the punter-returner, but before the punt (kick) is executed, these same *coverage men* primarily function as *blockers* (it's their first job to guard and protect the punter to ensure that he executes the punt without it getting blocked). Once the punter has kicked (punted) the football and the *blockers* hear the football kicked, they immediately shift their mindsets and their mission—they now become *coverage men*. This is a dual function of the special teams' players on the punt team. Remember, for the punt team, players are *blockers* for their own punter, and then *coverage men* against the opposing *punt-returner*.

Rushers are the special teams players who are responsible for rushing the blockers and attempting to block a kick, either on an extra-point attempt, field-goal attempt, or punt. The *rushers* try to defeat the opposing blockers to make a big play; conversely, the blockers try to ensure their block to avoid a big play and guarantee the execution of a clean kick. The *rushers* are generally role players.

Note: When *rushers* line up on the punt-return team, the end game is to block for the their own punt-returner, but before the opponents' punt (kick) is executed, these same *blockers* primarily function as *rushers* (it's their first job to rush and attempt to block the opposing punter's kick or, in many instances, fake as though they are trying to block the punter's kick).

Once the punter has kicked (punted) the football and the *rushers* hear the football kicked, they immediately shift their mindsets and their mission—they now become *blockers*. This is a dual-function of the special teams' players on the punt-return team. Remember, for the punt-return team, players are rushers against the opposing punter, and then blockers for their own punt-returner.

The **hands team** is a specialty group of members from the kickoff-return team; they are a collection of the absolute best hands on the team, designed specifically to secure the football on on-side kicks (usually when the opponents' kickoff team is making a trick kick out of desperation, intended for the opposing kickoff team to secure the football). The *hands team's* job is to catch the football, regardless of the conditions, circumstances, or of how hard they may get hit while in the process of trying to secure the football. The *hands team* is mostly made up of role players.

The **gunner (headhunter)** is the special teams player who lines up on the outside of the punt team, runs down the sidelines as quickly and athletically as possible to discourage the punt-returner from returning the punt, and when necessary, secures the tackle on the punt-returner. The *gunner* is generally a tenacious player, role player, and a team player all rolled up into one player. The *gunner* is normally *double-teamed* (two of the opponents' players line up in front of the *gunner* and try to inhibit his ability to get down the field and make a tackle on the punt-returner; 2 against 1). Because the *gunner* is such a tenacious player, he often beats the double-team and still makes tackles on the punt-returner. The gunners are primarily role players.

On-side kick team is a specialty group of the kickoff team that is specifically designed to target players on the opponents' hands team; Members of the *on-side kick team* will attempt to knock down players on the opposing hands team while other players on the *on-side kick team* try secure the **short trick kick**, which is intended to bounce in the air. In most instances, a coach will make a call for the special teams to execute an on-side kick in order to get the football back for their offensive team to make a comeback attempt. The *on-side kick team* is often made up of mostly role players.

As in many cases, there are exceptions to the general rule. For example, a coach with an aggressive approach and one of the greatest all-time **drop-a-set** (a full explanation of this phrase can be found in chapter 7, but the reference is often associated with being bold and brave, in the football vernacular) decisions for a special teams' play, especially in a Super Bowl, was when the New Orleans Saints' head coach in Super Bowl XLIV, made an over-the-top decision to call an on-side kick to start the second half, while the Saints were only trailing the Colts 6 to 10, a close game by any measure.

The Saints' on-side kick team caught the Indianapolis Colts' kick-off return team off-guard when they executed an on-side kick, and they secured the football. This was a great call, great execution, and one of the greatest special teams' plays in Super Bowl history.

Note: All of the different special teams' players for the various special teams are coached by a position coach that's called the **special teams coach**.

The special teams, like the offensive team and defensive team, uses **situational preparation** (planning and preparing for different situations by studying the opponents' personnel and tendencies) to prepare for their opponents' special teams. Usually, the special teams prepares from two perspectives; the first is based on the special teams' own philosophy, personnel, and game plan. The second is based on what their opponents' special teams' strengths and weaknesses are, as well as whether the opposing special teams takes a conservative approach or an aggressive approach. *Situational preparation* is done in the form of studying and reviewing the opponents' personnel and tendencies (what type of plays they prefer, when they like to run the plays, where on the field and how often the team likes to run certain plays). In *situational preparation*, the special teams tries to prepare for every possible situation and scenario it may encounter against the opponents' special teams.

The special teams is primarily made up of team players who are proud to function as role players. Most special teams' players have well-defined roles; there is occasionally a star player on the special teams.

A special teams' game plan is usually the coaches' plan of attack against the opposing special teams, designed with a strategy for utilizing kick returns, kick coverage, blocking for kickers, and attempting to block kicks. Some coaches will choose a conservative approach with their kick returns (**kick returns** are when the blockers try to guard or keep the opponents' coverage men from tackling their punt-returner or kickoff-returner) and an aggressive approach with their kick coverage (**kick coverage** is when the coverage men on either the punt team or kickoff team go down the football field to tackle the punt-returner or kickoff-returner). However, another coach may have a special teams' game plan that calls for an aggressive approach in the kick returns and a conservative approach in the kick coverage. Then there's another coach who has a special teams' game plan where he chooses a balanced attack in kick returns and kick coverage equally.

All of the plays that involve kicking the football—receiving and securing possession of the football when kicked, covering and tackling a kick-returner, and attempting to secure points by kicking—all constitute the **kicking game**.

The special teams is a type of transition team, achieving possession delivery and point delivery while one team transitions from their offensive team to their defensive team, and the opponents transition from their defensive team to their offensive team. The special teams delivers possession of the football on the kickoff team and punt team, and it receives possession of the football on the kickoff-return team, punt-return team, and hands team. The special teams delivers points when it maximizes scoring attempts on extra points and field goals.

My outlook of special teams' players is that they champion field position. There is often an under-appreciation for special teams' players and their impact on field position. So many observers do not realize that field position actually comes into play on every series that the offensive and defensive teams encounter. Interestingly enough, these special teams' players are viewed by many as understudy players or adjunct athletes for players on both the offensive team and the defensive team. The fact of the matter is, the special teams has just as much importance as the offensive team and defensive team in the grand scheme of things, particularly as it pertains to the 3 teams in 1. The players on both the offensive and defensive teams could not fully execute their roles and responsibilities without the play and execution of the special teams' players.

Neither the players from the offensive nor the defensive team could play as hard and execute 60 to 70 offensive and defensive plays, respectively, and then go out onto the field and have enough energy to execute the additional 15 to 30 special teams plays required over the course of an American football game. Indeed, the special teams is special because its players are specialists on the various special teams' units, just as the offensive players and defensive players are specialists for their respective teams. Also, the special teams' players are special because they are actually a type of field-position stylist.

In most cases, when the offensive team or defensive team starts their series with good field position or bad field position, it's the result of the play of the special teams. There is an exception when the defensive team forces the opponents' offensive team to commit a *turnover* (when the opponents' offensive team loses possession of the football by a fumble or an interception). Otherwise, the special teams creates the field position. Again, the special teams is a type of field-position stylist.

The special teams' players are sometimes viewed as the ***ghosts of gains*** in yards and territory. It's as if the fans can't see or don't know that the special teams actually produces the results in field position. In American football, field position is something the casual observer misses, misinterprets, or does not understand. There is a more detailed explanation of the different areas or zones on the football field in chapter 8.

There are many who see special teams' players purely as backup players who are happy to get onto the playing field or happy to get their 30 seconds of fame. I suggest that those who hold those views about special teams' players back up and get a better grasp on the facts as they relate to the importance of field position as well as the actual impact that field position has on the outcome of many games. When it comes to impacting field position, the special teams is second to none. It's champ or chomp, best or bust. Again, every sequence, down, and play in American football has a winner and loser. When the players on the special teams champion field position, it's a win for the entire team.

The overall play and execution of the special teams is a type of facelift for the offensive team and defensive team. Because the special teams is a type of g stylist, their execution gives the offensive and defensive teams a good look or a bad look as it pertains to field position.

There are **4 Key Indicators for Success for the Special Teams**:

1. ***Maximize Kick Returns***: When the special teams has success on the punt-return team and the kick-returns teams, it helps in the overall outcome of the game. *Maximizing kick returns* is a key indicator for success for the special teams.
2. ***Maximize Kick Coverage***: When the special teams has success on the punt team and kickoff team, it helps in the overall outcome of the game. *Maximizing kick coverage* is a key indicator for success for the special teams.
3. ***Maximize Scoring Attempts***: When the special teams has success on the extra-point/field-goal teams, it helps in the overall outcome of the game. *Maximizing scoring attempts* is a key indicator for success for the special teams.
4. ***Protecting Possession of the Football***: When the special teams has success in protecting possession of the football on kickoff returns, punt returns, and the hands team, it helps in the overall outcome of the game. Maximizing *protecting possession of the football* is a key indicator for success for the special teams.

The play and performance of the special teams is at its best when it complements their offensive team by maximizing *kick returns* (punt returns and kickoff returns). When the special teams has success in kick returns, it helps its offensive team by putting them in good field position. Note: After the special teams executes kick returns, the offensive team takes the field.

The play and performance of the special teams is at its best when it complements its defensive team by maximizing *kick coverage* (punt team and kickoff team). When the special teams has success in kick coverage, it helps its defensive team by putting the opponents' offensive team in poor or bad field position. Note: After the special teams executes kick coverage, the defensive team goes onto the football field.

The play and performance of the special teams is at its best when it complements the offensive team and defensive team by maximizing *scoring attempts* (extra-point and field-goal attempts). When the special teams has success in securing scoring attempts, it helps its offensive team by adding to the point total and creating a greater point margin for the opponents' offensive team to overcome or reducing a lead by the opponents' offensive team. It also helps its defensive team by adding to the point total, creating a greater point margin and allowing the defensive team to play more aggressively, or conversely, by reducing the opponents' lead and energizing the defensive team with a smaller point margin to defend against any future scoring attempts by the opposing offensive team.

The play and performance of the special teams is at its best when it complements its offensive team by *protecting possession of the football*. When the special teams protects possession of the football, it helps its offensive team by ensuring them an additional possession of the football to have another opportunity to attempt to gain territory and score.

It's often demoralizing and deflates the energy of a lot of teams when their special teams—in particular the kickoff-return team, punt-return team, punt team, and field-goal team—commit a *turnover* (when a team loses possession of the football by means of a fumble or interception to the opponent). In most cases, when the special teams commits a turnover, it's a fumble, with the exception of the punt team on a fake punt or the field-goal team on a fake field goal, if they attempt a pass that's intercepted by the defensive team. When the special teams protects possession of the football, it is effective in executing the transition of possession.

Indeed, the special teams is expected to be a *field-position creator* and a *point creator* by putting both their offensive team and defensive team in good field position and by securing points on scoring attempts. No doubt you are watching football at its best when one unit compliments another unit. The success of the special teams certainly complements the success of both the offensive team and defensive team.

Phase 2

CHAPTER 5

Locker Room

Bedroom

*T*he **locker room** is the super jock's sanctuary; it's like a land of its own. There is much action that takes place in the *locker room* of an American football team, especially from the high-school football level all the way through the professional football level.

Many personalities and attitudes coincide in this special space for football players. The locker room is where the many talents, personalities, and alliances coexist. Generally, what occurs in the locker room stays in the locker room—i.e., What happens in the locker room is nobody's business but the teammates who are in the locker room when it happens. It's similar to the personal space of your bedroom—what happens in your bedroom is nobody's business but yours.

Let's explore some locker-room scenes and situations in what I call the ***Land of the Locker Room***:

In the Land of the Locker Room, there is **locker-room business**. First and foremost, when each player enters the locker room, his primary focus is football business. Although players intermingle with one another, each player knows that when he enters the locker room, it's a new day and there are new tasks at hand with regards to getting better as a team—this goes for the offensive team, defensive team, and special teams.

In the same way, the business of relationship teams has precedence with regards to making their relationship team better.

In the Land of the Locker Room, there is **locker-room camaraderie**. This is a result of players learning to trust one another; they also see each other as family. In *locker-room camaraderie*, team unity is developed, and players feel connected because of their mutual mission—their team goals.

Relationship teams also develop a type of camaraderie as a result of each member trusting one another; a unity develops among them, and the members feel connected because of their joint effort in pursuing their relationship goals.

In the Land of the Locker Room, there is a **locker-room culture**. Team players and star players discuss things from their meeting room regarding their game plan, as well as their upcoming opponents. They also discuss issues and concerns that should be addressed on the practice field. The team captains and team leaders make sure each player maintains a certain focus in the locker room at the appropriate times.

In the Land of the Locker Room, there is **locker-room loyalty**. Teammates see themselves as brothers. They stick together through thick and thin, and they fight together and support one another. The *us against them* mentality evolves through *locker-room loyalty*.

Relationship teams benefit from this type of loyalty, sticking together through thick and thin, providing endless support for each member.

In the Land of the Locker Room, there is **locker-room etiquette**. Every player in the locker room has his own space—his own locker. It's understood that you respect each player's personal space. No player in the locker room is worried or concerned with having his personal belongings taken or stolen. It's understood that nobody touches anyone else's personal belongings for any reason, under any condition.

For example, in the NFL, players are comfortable and do not think twice about leaving valuables in their lockers. In fact, there are players in the NFL who will leave $1,000 cash in their pockets or wallets while attending meetings or going out onto the practice field.

In the Land of the Locker Room, there are **locker-room alliances**. In many instances, a player will form alliances with those players whose lockers are next to his own locker—his neighbors. A player will also form alliances with teammates who play the same position. Occasionally there are players from the same college, city, or state who form alliances.

In the Land of the Locker Room, there are **locker-room fellowships**. There are certain players who eat together on a regular basis. When I played in the NFL, there were three other teammates and myself who ate lunch together regularly throughout the season.

In the Land of the Locker Room, there are **locker-room cliques**. There are instances in the locker room where some of the backup players are not allowed in some of the inner circles of the starting players. This is also true in the reverse—there are instances when some of the backup players who want to feel empowered have their own inner circles, and they refuse to interact with some of the starting players.

In the Land of the Locker Room, there is a **locker-room play-by-play announcer**. There's usually one player in the locker room who, regardless of what happens, chooses to take a sports announcer's approach to make sure everyone in the locker room notices a particular incident. He will bring attention to any incident he considers noteworthy in an entertaining and descriptive way as he frames it as a football play.

In the Land of the Locker Room, there are **locker-room numbers**. Each player's number is on everything, starting with his locker. A player's number will also appear on his jersey, practice gear, folders, backpack, gym bag, etc.

A player identifies with whatever his number is; for example, I wore number 27 when I played with the New Orleans Saints. Every time I see anything with the number 27 on it, I do a double take. The number 27 is a number I will always identify with everywhere I go.

In the Land of the Locker Room, there is **locker-room support**. Players receive an enormous amount of support from the locker room for all personal matters regarding family or personal challenges.

In the Land of the Locker Room, there is a **locker-room leak**. The only way the media or anyone outside of the team is aware of locker-room matters or family matters is when one of the players is their source, or the *locker-room leak*. The majority of players starting at the high-school football level know how important it is to keep the locker-room matters in-house. Unfortunately, most football teams have a *locker-room leak*.

In the Land of the Locker Room, there are **locker-room fights**. Normally, in most locker rooms, there is at least one physical fight over the course of a football season. And verbal fights are a regular occurrence.

In the Land of the Locker Room, there is a **locker-room bully**. Having a bully in the locker room is probably most prevalent in middle-school football and high-school football. Certainly there are *locker-room* *bullies* in college football and professional football as well. It's as if these guys are hooked up to a constant drip of testosterone.

I can recall an incident in college football when I transferred from the University of Arkansas football team to the University of Memphis football team, where I was threatened and challenged by the *locker-room bully*. Maybe since I was quiet and reserved, this *locker-room bully* misinterpreted it as my being timid or someone he could intimidate.

I had previously observed the bullying in other instances with a couple of other players. When this bully approached and threatened me, I quickly informed him, "Where I come from, we don't do all of that talking. If you want to do something, let's do it. I'm cool with fighting if that's what you want, but I don't do all of that talking. What do you want to do?" Well, that fight never materialized.

In the Land of the Locker Room, there are **locker-room legends**. There is at least one player on every football team who does something so spectacular, so phenomenal, so outrageous, or so amazing that he instantly becomes a *locker-room legend*. And his teammates remember this player and this incident forever.

In the Land of the Locker Room, there is **locker-room privacy**. As far as players are concerned, what goes on in the locker room, stays in the locker room, and what's said in the locker room, stays in the locker room.

In the Land of the Locker Room, as it pertain to locker-room visitors, simply put—No Visitors Allowed!

In the Land of the Locker Room, regarding **locker-room hygiene**: Invariably, every football team, starting as early as middle-school football and going all the way up to professional football, there will always be a couple of teammates who wear so much cologne it's as if they actually bathe in it. I call them cologne chokers because they put on so much cologne that when they walk by you, the smell chokes you and leaving you gasping for air.

There are also wind-breakers. These are players who are proud to be the ones to release clouds of foul odors throughout the locker room, imposing temporary discomfort to their teammates' sense of smell. As a result, they cause their teammates to temporarily disown them, while recommending that they seek medical treatment.

In the Land of the Locker Room, there are **locker-room exhibitionists**. For some reason, most football teams have a few players who really like to see themselves bare, in their birthday suits. Perhaps they are misguided in thinking their teammates are cool with their exhibitionist mentality. They move through the locker room free and clear, with no resolve as it pertains to getting dressed.

In the Land of the Locker Room, there's an occasional **locker-room shower saga**. Occasionally, players are confused by certain things that go on in the locker room. I can recall players asking the question on two separate occasions, somewhere between high-school football and professional football. Why is our teammate getting excited in the shower?

This *locker-room shower saga* left me saying, "Really! Really! Really! Really! Really! Really! Really! Really! Really! Really! Naaaaah. No way. Really! Really! Really! Really! Really! Really! Really! Really! Really! Really! Ah DANG!!!"

In the Land of the Locker Room, there are **locker-room weigh-ins**. *Locker-room weigh-ins* take place particularly in college football and professional football.

In the NFL, most teams have a weigh-in on Friday mornings. All players are required to maintain a certain weight or are allowed a certain weight range. That's right—you have a group of men whose identity is attached to their body mass.

There are always a couple of players who will try anything to shed those last couple of pounds to make their weight and avoid receiving the fines associated with being overweight. I do mean anything—like going into the restroom and forcing the #2 (yeah, that's right, the good old #2). They make a last-ditch effort to shed those last couple of pounds. I guess this gives new meaning to calling an *audible*, as well as, oh let's say, taking an *aggressive approach*.

In the Land of the Locker Room, there is **locker-room laughter**. When it's not time to deal with the business of playing football, the locker room is one of the funniest places ever. In some instances, during downtime in a football locker room, there is nonstop laughter—in fact, boisterous laughter.

There's an ancient adage that says that laughter is like a medicine and it does the body good. There are times when *locker-room laughter* can ease stress and frustration that teams sometimes experience.

Although there are usually several players who produce *locker-room laughter*, there's at least one guy on every football team who has potential to do stand-up comedy. He's naturally funny, has great delivery, and never runs out of material. He's the mainstay when it comes to *locker-room laughter*.

In the Land of the Locker Room, there are **locker-room secrets**. Sorry, I can't tell you anything here—it's a SECRET!!!

In the Land of the Locker Room, you hear many voices—voices of hope, joy, doubt, pain, and triumph. In the Land of the Locker Room, you see the blood, sweat, and tears shed by an array of talents. In the Land of the Locker Room, you can experience the touch of teamwork and of team unity as a team moves toward their team goals. In the Land of the Locker Room, you can smell the sweat of the hard work that comes with an intense pursuit of team goals. In the Land of the Locker Room, you feel the sting of setbacks and the distress of defeat. Conversely, you feel the enjoyment of winning and the thrill of triumph.

There are so many different talents and personalities that coincide within this room. The role players, star players, confident players, cocky players, tenacious players, timid players, selfish players, verbal leaders, and the players who lead by example find ways to coexist in respect, brotherhood, and unity while in the Land of the Locker Room.

Similarly, relationship teams that are successful, find ways to coexist in respect, partnership, and unity.

CHAPTER 6

Huddle

Circle of Communication

A **huddle** is where a team or a certain number of teammates gather together in an organized manner to communicate. A *huddle* has a two-fold purpose: one, to execute **secret communication**, and two, to execute the **call for the next play**.

The *secret communication* of the huddle is significant because it's vital that the opponents do not hear the play call. Normally, when the offensive team is in their huddle, the quarterback will have his back toward the line of scrimmage and the opponents' defensive team as he makes the play call in the offensive huddle. As for the defensive team, if the middle linebacker is the **signal caller** (the player who is designated to call the play in the huddle), he will have his back toward the line of scrimmage and the opponents' offensive team as he makes the play call in the defensive huddle. Neither *signal caller* wants to be heard or have his lips read by the opponents.

The *huddle* is also essential as an assembly for the players to make the *call for the next play*. After each play is executed, specifically by the offensive team and defensive team, a huddle is formed to communicate the *call for the next play*. The huddle is significant because it symbolizes a **circle of communication**. This communication is imperative to ensuring that each player is on the same page with regards to the *call for the next play*.

Although the special teams have a huddle for the *call for the next play*, in most instances, the special teams do not have back-to-back plays to execute. Usually, they execute a play and then go to the sidelines. (For example, the punt team, kickoff team, extra-point team, etc., each have a specific play that they implement, and then they return to the sidelines.) In many instances, the special teams will have a sideline huddle, and occasionally, they will huddle on the field in front of the football.

Note: The *signal caller* is the player who is responsible for calling the play (signal) in the huddle, for each team. The *signal caller* for the offensive team is always the quarterback. In most cases, the middle linebacker is the *signal caller* for the defensive team. There is also a designated *signal caller* for the special teams; generally, it's the player who the special teams coach trusts the most.

Remember, the *signal caller* for each of the teams (the offensive team, defensive team, and special teams) is the one and only voice in the huddle—the only player designated to speak. All of the other 10 players are coached to look only at the signal caller, listen closely, and be quiet while in the huddle whenever the signal caller is speaking. Furthermore, the signal caller is coached to speak loudly, speak clearly, and repeat every play call in the huddle to ensure that his teammates hear the *call for the next play*. After the signal caller has repeated the play call in the huddle, other players are permitted to make comments or ask questions.

Before every game, each team's captain(s) and the referee huddle at midfield for a **coin toss**. The *coin toss* is when the referee flips a coin up in the air (one side with heads and the other side with tails), and the visiting team's captain is allowed to call heads or tails. If the visiting captain wins the coin toss, he communicates to the referee whether his team is going to:

1. Receive the football via a **kickoff return**. (With this option, the visiting team receives the football at the beginning of the first half. They will not receive the football at the beginning of the second half.)

2. Execute a **kickoff** and decline to receive the football first until after the halftime break. (When the visiting team elects to receive the football at the beginning of the second half instead of receiving the football at the beginning of the game, they are also making the decision to execute a *kickoff*; as a result, the home team would have to execute a *kickoff return*.)

Although the game has four quarters, it's divided up into two halves—the **first half** and the **second half**—with a **halftime** break in between the two. During the *halftime* break, each team goes to its designated locker room, where they take a short break and make adjustments in their strategies for the second half. They make corrections for the plays they made mistakes on in the first half, in the hopes that the adjustments will generate more-efficient execution in the second half. In some instances, the players recognize the mistakes they made on certain plays in the first half.

Initially, the team will *huddle* as a group to hear comments, encouragement, critiques, frustration, and direction from the head coach. Then the team will *huddle* separately as a defensive team and as an offensive team to hear from the defensive coordinator and offensive coordinator, respectively (remember, the two coordinators are the coaches who direct and manage the entire offensive and defensive teams). As the teams are broken up into defensive and offensive teams, the players also *huddle* up by position.

For example, all of the linebackers will huddle together beside the linebackers coach, all of the defensive linemen will huddle up together beside the defensive line coach. And all of the defensive backs will huddle up together beside the defensive backs coach. Then the defensive coordinator gives his comments, encouragement, critiques, frustration, and direction. Then each position coach on the defensive team is allocated a few minutes with his players to give comments, encouragement, critiques, frustration, corrections, and direction. And sometimes, depending on the amount of time left for the halftime break, the defensive captain may huddle up with the entire defensive team for a few words of exhortation before going back out onto the football field.

The same is true for the offensive team. The players also huddle by position. For example, all of the running backs huddle together beside the running backs coach; all of the offensive linemen huddle together beside the offensive line coach. And so on—the quarterbacks huddle together beside the quarterbacks coach and the wide receivers huddle together beside the receivers coach. The offensive coordinator gives his comments, encouragement, critiques, frustration, corrections, and direction, and then each position coach on the offensive team is allotted a few minutes with his players to give comments, encouragement, critiques, frustration, corrections, and direction. Like the defensive captain, the offensive captain may huddle up with the entire offensive team for a few words of encouragement before going back onto the football field.

And in many instances, all of the assistant coaches will huddle up with the head coach, sometimes before they meet with the players, and sometimes after they meet with the players just before they head back out onto the football field for the second half. Note: There are always huddles going on somewhere with a football team.

Officials often *huddle* to make sure the right call has been made, and also to make certain that there's clarity on a call—in particular when two different officials are making a different call with regards to a penalty or infraction on a particular play.

I have a major recommendation for you regarding the officials, penalties, and infractions—specifically regarding the notion of learning all of the penalties and infractions in American football. As an alternative, I recommend learning only two rules—I call them "RJ's Rules," or "Reggie Jones' Rules."

RJ's Rule #1: Throw in the white towel on the yellow flag. (The penalty marker in American football, the **yellow flag** is thrown on the field to indicate that a penalty or an infraction has occurred).

FYI, not every player on every football team knows all of the rules. Having said that, why stress over knowing all of the rules? (By the way, if I was interested in discussing rules and penalties with you, that would be a separate book altogether.) Please do NOT concern yourself with learning or trying to learn all of the penalties and infractions in American football.

It's also important to note that you have an unidentified advantage when watching an American football game on television, both at the college-football and professional-football levels. When there is a yellow flag on the football field for a penalty/infraction, you can listen carefully to the sports announcer for assistance. The sports announcer will always give an explanation of the penalty/infraction, as well as tell you which player committed the infraction. Remember *RJs Rule #1*: Throw in the white towel regarding learning all of the rules/penalties/infractions in American football.

RJ's Rule # 2: When you're watching a football game on TV and there is a yellow flag on the football field, listen carefully to the sports announcer for an explanation of the penalty, as well as who committed the infraction.

And if you generally attend games at the middle-school and high-school levels and do not watch football on television, yet you're interested in learning more about the penalties, I would strongly recommend watching a few games on TV over the course of the season and applying "RJ's Rules." Doing so will certainly give you some idea of what's going on in relation to the penalties/infractions associated with the **yellow flag**.

Effective communication is paramount to the success of every American football team, starting with little-league football teams, middle-school football teams, high-school football teams, college football teams, and especially professional football teams.

Effective communication in American football is the catalyst for a successful strategy and a prerequisite to excellent execution. *Effective communication* is the catalyst for a successful strategy because, if the strategy is not communicated clearly, competently, and confidently, the likelihood of it being heard and received is greatly diminished. Ultimately, this would impact the implementation of the team's strategy/game plan.

Effective communication for a football team is a prerequisite to excellent execution because it simply is not possible to have excellent execution on any given play if all 11 players are not on the same page, and that starts with *effective communication*.

Effective communication is just as vital for a relationship team as it is to the success of a football team. *Effective communication* is also a catalyst for a successful strategy for relationship teams, and it also serves as a prerequisite to excellent execution for a relationship team. Each member of the relationship team has to hear and receive the strategy for the relationship team clearly, competently, and confidently, as well as be on the same page in order to execute their team goals in excellence.

On the contrary, when a football team has **ineffective communication**, every member of the team is not clear, competent, or confident in the strategy/game plan—in this case, failure is certain. Also, when the prerequisite to excellent execution has not been met, excellent execution is absolutely stifled. *Ineffective communication* for a football team leads to inconsistent performances and improbable success.

Similar to a football team, *ineffective communication* will result in each member of a relationship team not being clear, competent, or confident in the strategy for the relationship team—again, in this case, failure is certain. Also, failing to meet the prerequisite of *effective communication* will diminish any chance of excellent execution for the relationship team.

Football teams also apply both **verbal communication** and **nonverbal communication**. The process of using *verbal communication* is essential to having a success strategy for every football team. How well a head coach and his assistant coaches communicate their strategy/game plan is paramount to the success of the team. The clearer their *verbal communication* is, the more likely it is received, and it leads to excellent execution from each team (the offensive team, defensive team, and special teams).

In addition, the clearer the *verbal communication* is for a relationship team, the more likely it is received by each member of the relationship team. Of all the ways to deal with and overcome challenges to a relationship team, *verbal communication* is the most favorable. *Verbal communication* gives relationship teams the impetus to produce successful strategies and excellent execution of the relationship team goals.

Players on the offensive team, defensive team, and special teams learn to implement and utilize *non-verbal communication* as a result of the impact of crowd noise. During the course of an American football game, players use *non-verbal communication* in the form of gestures and hand signals to get their message across in the midst of extremely loud crowd noise.

Like football teams, there are times when a relationship team finds themselves needing to utilize *non-verbal communication* while in the midst of crowd noises (those who are loud and noisy in opposition to the success of the relationship team). And, like a football team, a relationship team can benefit from learning to implement and utilize *non-verbal communication* in the form of gestures and signals in order to get their message through to each member in the midst of crowd noises.

Again, the *huddle* is significant because it symbolizes a *circle of communication*. This communication is imperative to the success of every American football team, as well as to ensuring that each player is on the same page. Remember, a *huddle* is where a team or a certain number of teammates gather together in an organized manner to communicate. Again, a *huddle* has a two-fold purpose: one, to execute *secret communication*, and two, to execute the *call for the next play*.

After every game, win or lose, the entire football team will *huddle* in the locker room. On the occasions following a win, the team will hear words of encouragement and congratulatory comments from their head coach. However, in instances following a loss—especially depending on how hard the team played in their defeat—the team will often hear a scolding monologue of disapproval or of hopeful resolve for improvement before the next game.

The use of the huddle or circle of communication extends from the locker room to the sidelines to the playing field as the main method of communication for an American football team.

Phase 3

CHAPTER 7

Strategy

Rules of Engagement

*T*he **strategy** that a *head football coach* implements has everything to do with how competitive and how successful a football team will be. The onus is on the head coach to design the right *strategy*. Every coach has a basic philosophy of how he will approach each opponent, each game. Typically based on the strengths and weaknesses of the opposing team, the coach will make adjustments in the schemes, or tweak them. In some instances, the opponents' strength could be a challenge, so the coach will spend more time preparing in this area of anticipated challenge. On the flip side, the opponents' area of weakness could be an area to exploit. So, the *strategy* would be to emphasize to the team that this is an area or phase of the game where they must dominate their opponents.

The primary responsibilities of the **head coach** are getting the football team prepared in terms of knowing and understanding both their game plan and their opponents, as well as getting the team prepared to execute their game efficiently against those opponents. The coaching responsibilities are shared with the offensive coordinator and defensive coordinator, as well as other assistant football coaches—position coaches. The bottom line is, the *head coach* is the architect of the game plan.

The **coin toss** is when a coin is flipped in the air before the game to determine who receives the football first. A *strategy* that many coaches use is that if they are playing a home game, they defer receiving the football until after halftime (the second half) and start the game with their defensive team. They want to use their defensive team to set the tempo of the game, as well as get the crowd into the game. However, if a team has an offensive team that's simply one of the best in their respective leagues, the team would likely elect to start the game with the offensive team. And the opposite is generally true if it's a road game. Many coaches will elect to receive the football and start the game with their offensive team. The objective with this *strategy* is to try to get points up on the scoreboard first on a road game in an effort to neutralize the crowd in a hostile environment.

The coaches organize the team's strategy in the form of a **game plan**, a plan they all feel is a roadmap to success. This is also referred to as a football team's **plan of attack**. The offensive team, defensive team, and special teams each have a *plan of attack* designed specifically for them.

All football teams have a plan of attack. Some teams will go after the opponents' weakest unit or weakest player(s)—with the objective of gaining territory and ultimately scoring. For example, if the opponents' defensive end (DE) is a great pass rusher, but he's the defensive team's weakest link as far as their rushing defense is concerned, an offensive team strategy may be to *double-team* (when a team assigns two blockers to one player—it's two versus one) this defensive end (DE) on most of the passing plays in order to stop him from putting too much pressure on or *sacking* their quarterback (QB) (remember that *sacking* the quarterback means tackling or taking him down to the ground behind the line of scrimmage, which would result in a loss of yards).

And on the flip side, because he is the defensive team's weakest link on running plays, the strategy would be to run most of their running plays directly at this defensive end (DE). As a result, they are confident they will have success against him on running plays or in the *running game.*

In some cases, the offensive team's strategy may be to implement 10% to 20% more running plays because their opponents' *run defense* is so weak. Likewise, if it's the opponents' *pass defense* that is weak, then the strategy for the offensive team may be to implement 10% to 20% more passing plays.

Sometimes it's the offensive team's strategy or defensive team's strategy to highlight their own strength. In this case, the team is not concerned with the opponents' weakness—their objective is simply to highlight and play to their own strengths. For example, if the offensive team's strength is the *running game*, then they will go into the game with a strategy to run the football the majority of the time in order to highlight and rely on their own strength. They will use their success in the *running game* to open up opportunities and have success in the *passing game* as the defensive team has to make adjustments to slow down or stop the success of their *running game*. Usually in the process of making adjustments, many times the defensive team will become vulnerable in their *pass defense*. This vulnerability is created as a result of the defensive team overcompensating or over-committing players to try to stop from being dominated against the opponents' *running game*.

In American football, teams routinely face a variety of situations in each game—some expected and some unexpected. Again, this requires what's called *situational preparation*. Teams usually practice on different situations based on the **tendencies** (what type of plays the opponents run, how often the opponents run the plays, when the opponents run the plays, and what location on the field they typically run certain plays) the opponents have, whether they be on the offensive team, defensive team, or special teams.

So, the offensive team would look at film of the opponents' defensive team's previous games to study their *tendencies* and practice against those *tendencies*. The defensive team would look at film of the opponents' offensive team's previous games to study their *tendencies* and practice against those *tendencies*. The special teams would look at film of the opponents' special teams' previous games to study their *tendencies* and practice against those *tendencies*. (Special teams' *tendencies* for the punt team, punt-return team, kickoff team, kickoff-return team, extra-point team, field-goal team, on-side kick team, and hands team are all reviewed, studied, and practiced.)

Tendencies are usually based on *down* and *distance*. (For example, if a team has 1st & 10, the 1st represents the first of 4 possible downs, and the 10 represents 10 yards to go to secure the next 1st & 10. Each time an offensive team gets or *secures a 1st down* or 1st & 10, they earn 4 new downs/4 new attempts, or a new set of downs. This is a process the offensive team would like to repeat over and over, in order to gain territory and ultimately score.) When a defensive team is studying the opposing offensive team's tendencies, they are looking to see what the offensive team likes to do on different *downs* and *distances*. For example, in the instances when the opponents' offensive team has a 3rd & 3 (meaning 3rd down and 3 yards to go or to gain in order to secure a 1st down), they notice the offensive team has a tendency to run the football up the middle. Tendencies are also determined by *field position* and *personnel*. For example, let's say the opponents are close to scoring a touchdown. They are 12 yards away from the end zone. They have a 1st down and 10 yards to go; film study reveals that the opponents have a *tendency* to put 4 receivers in the game in this scenario. In this case, the *tendencies* reveal something relevant with regards to *field position* (in this case, the team is in the red zone—within 20 yards of the end zone), and with regards to *personnel* (the opponent likes to use 4 receivers inside of the red zone area).

In a similar fashion, relationship teams can benefit when each member learns and understands their own *tendencies*, as well as the *tendencies* of their teammate. Understanding the *tendencies* for the relationship team will put both of the parties involved in a better position to be prepared to handle the various situations they might encounter, in the game of life or in the game of love.

As discussed in chapters 2, 3, and 4, every coach has his **rules of engagement** laid out in his *game plan*, also known as his *plan of attack*. And so it is with the offensive team, defensive team, and special teams.

Generally speaking, most football coaches are risk-averse. In American football, there are two different types of coaches: one who takes a conservative approach and another who takes an aggressive approach.

The **conservative approach** is when the coach calls for safe plays; essentially, the *conservative approach* is coaching and playing not to lose the game. The **aggressive approach** is when the coach makes aggressive calls for aggressive and risky plays; consequently the *aggressive approach* is coaching and playing to win the game.

If you take an opinion poll with American football players and ask them, if they had the option in a close game, would they prefer to support a coach whose strategy is to take a conservative approach that ultimately results in losing the game, or a coach whose strategy takes an aggressive approach, and they try everything possible to win the game, though the result is still losing the game, an overwhelming majority of players would pick the coach who takes the aggressive approach.

Players, without doubt, are more frustrated and dejected when they lose a game and they know their coach did not do or risk everything possible to try to win the game because of a conservative approach. In these instances, there are usually several players on the team who will say to their teammates that the coach needs to **drop-a-set**. By saying *drop-a-set*, these players are referring to the twin pair of male private parts, often associated with being bold and brave in football vernacular.

Now, on the other hand, if a coach tries everything, explores every opportunity and takes maximal risks, and the result is still losing the game, the players will come out saying, "We tried everything possible, and we left everything on the field. The team that played the best won today— we'll get them the next time." Players cope with losing better when they know that their coaches and their teammates did everything they could to try to win the game.

Players have a hard time overlooking a loss as a result of a coach being too conservative. Players always esteem a coach who champions virility in decisive moments. Players prefer a more gonadic tactic, favoring a head coach having a testosterone release in the heat of the battle, as opposed to a head coach who exhibits the parody of a maternal persona.

I think a conservative approach and coaching football is like an oxymoron. And I certainly do not believe that playing smart football and playing conservative football is synonymous. You can definitely play smart football with an aggressive approach, as proven by Super Bowl–winning coaches of the New Orleans Saints, Green Bay Packers, New England Patriots, Indianapolis Colts, Pittsburgh Steelers, and New York Giants.

Similar to football teams, members of a relationship team take a conservative approach or an aggressive approach with regards to their *rules of engagement* for their relationship team. Certainly with relationship teams, there's a time and place for either approach.

It's extremely important to **respect your opponents**. Players, who do not respect their opponents usually do not adequately prepare for them. A player has to properly prepare for his opponents in order to execute well against them. Having a healthy respect for your opponents, yet never fearing your opponents, is the right strategy for preparing for an opposing team.

There are always football teams that feel they are superior to certain opponents. Although some teams are better coached and have more talent than others, the moment a football team disrespects another team and does not properly prepare to execute efficiently against them, they are setting themselves up for an upset. When a team actually has more talent than their opponent, disrespects them, takes them for granted, and ends up going into the game unprepared, a loss is inevitable.

Let's recap for a moment: There are several **factors in play calling**— *down, distance, field position, time,* and *score.* Note: Each of the three teams have a strategy regarding how to handle and approach these different factors in terms of their abilities in order to execute efficiently.

Again, the *down* is a factor in play calling. The offensive team has possession of the football; the offense gets four *downs* (attempts) to gain 10 yards, which signifies 1st down or 1st & 10. The first attempt is 1st down, the second attempt is 2nd down, the third attempt is 3rd down, and if the offensive team elects to make a fourth attempt, the fourth attempt is 4th down. The defensive team determines if they are going to be conservative or aggressive against the opponents' running game or passing game.

In many instances, if an offensive team does not gain 10 yards by the 3rd down (gaining 10 yards would restart the sequence of a new set of downs, meaning four new downs, and a new attempt to get a 1st down at a new yard line), the team will elect to **punt** the football (kick it to the opponent on 4th down). This is where the special teams come into play. In this scenario, the **punt team** would come into the game and *punt* the football, with the objective of giving their defensive team an advantage by putting the opponent in bad or poor field position.

Distance is also a factor in play calling. *Distance* indicates how far the offensive team has to go on either set of downs to gain a total of 10 yards in order to secure a 1st down or 1st & 10. Getting or securing a 1st down, or 1st & 10, means gaining a total of at least 10 yards. Although an offensive team is allowed 4 downs or 4 attempts to do this (gain 10 yards for a 1st down), most offensive teams will only take the 1st down, 2nd down, and 3rd down to try; and in most cases, they will elect to punt the football on 4th down. For example, on 1st down or the 1st attempt, the offensive team gains 4 yards (because 4 yards of the 10 yards needed have been earned, this creates a 2nd down & 6). On 2nd down or the 2nd attempt, the offensive team gains 3 yards (because the 4 yards previously gained and now the 3 additional yards gained total 7 yards, this creates a 3rd down & 3). Then on the 3rd down or 3rd attempt, the offensive team gains 3 yards, so they get or secure a 1st down (the previous 7 yards—totaled from the 1st down and 2nd down—are now added to the 3 yards on 3rd down, which equals 10 yards—the amount needed for a 1st down or 1st & 10. Remember, each time an offensive team gets or secures a 1st down or 1st & 10, they earn 4 new downs (4 new attempts) or a new set of downs. This is a process the offensive team would like to repeat over and over, in order to gain territory and ultimately score. Again, based on the *distance*, the defensive team will take a conservative or aggressive approach toward the opponents' running game or passing game.

Field position is a factor in play calling. *Field position* is the location on the football field where a team takes possession of the football. An offensive team typically views field position from the standpoint of their starting position and how far it is from the end zone. Just as bad *field position* significantly reduces scoring opportunities, the opposite is also true—good *field position* significantly increases scoring opportunities. In many instances, the defensive team will apply defensive pressure on the opponents' offensive team when they are in bad field position. On the other hand, the defensive team will take a more conservative approach when the opponents' offensive team is in good field position.

Time is a factor in play calling. The *time* on the game clock is always a significant factor in how a head coach executes his game plan. When the score is either close or tied, and there's plenty of time left on the game clock, most coaches will stick to the script. However, when there isn't a lot of time left in the game, the offensive team will have a sense of urgency to hold onto a lead—if they are winning. On the other hand, the offensive team will have a sense of urgency to make a comeback if they are losing.

Likewise, the defensive team will take a more conservative approach when their team is winning the game and there is limited time left on the game clock. On the flip side, if they are losing the game with a limited amount of time left on the game clock, the defensive team will take a more aggressive approach; they will take a lot of risks to try to get the football back for their offensive team to attempt a comeback. In addition, the special teams will take more risks when their team is in a comeback scenario.

The *score* on the scoreboard is a factor in play calling, and it has a tremendous impact on how coaches call the game. For example, if the score is tied or close, a coach who normally takes a conservative approach will continue to remain conservative throughout the course of the game. However, if this coach and team are behind with a limited amount of time left on the scoreboard, then, all of the sudden, this coach will adjust his philosophy and take on an aggressive approach to try to generate a comeback and win the game.

Contrast that with the coach who normally takes an aggressive approach; he will stay aggressive when the score is tied or close and there is plenty of time left on the scoreboard. But if this team and coach has a lead on the scoreboard, and there is a limited amount of time left in the game, this coach who normally takes an aggressive approach will adjust his philosophy and take on a conservative approach to try to preserve the lead and ultimately win the game.

When a coach chooses to **feature** a star player, this means that the coach has designed a significant portion of his *game plan* around this star player. For example, let's say one of the star players is the halfback (HB). The game plan may call for the halfback (HB) to carry/run the football 25 to 30 times over the course of the game. So, if the offensive team finishes the game with a total of 60 offensive plays, the halfback (HB) would have accounted for just about half of the offensive plays in that game—he was *featured*.

Let's say the star player was a receiver and the coach decided to *feature* him. The game plan may call for the receiver to have 10 to 15 passes thrown to him over the course of the game. Generally speaking, the receiver doesn't get as many plays as the halfback (HB) when he is *featured*. One reason may be due to the fact that, on average, more receivers usually play in a game than running backs, so there's a greater distribution of the football to a number of players on passing plays versus running plays. For example, there may be three running backs who play in a game; conversely, there may be five to six receivers who play in the same game.

Remember, there are three types of plays an offensive team may use over the course of a game, or some variation of the three types of plays:

- *Power play*: The team is saying, "We are bigger and stronger than you and will overpower you—we will manhandle you." *Power plays* are more of a one-dimensional approach.
- *Isolation play*: The offensive team has determined that there's a specific weakness or weak players on the defensive team—usually because these players are weaker or less skilled; if possible, the offensive team will exploit these players over and over again. Likewise, a defensive team discovers certain weaknesses regarding certain players on the offensive team. The strategy would be to exploit these particular players. *Isolation plays* are also more of a one-dimensional approach.
- *Setup play*: Sometimes the offensive team will run certain plays over and over to get the defensive team into a certain frame of mind and in a certain position on the field, but they will then later run offensive plays to counter what the defensive team has adjusted to. These types of *setup plays* are very strategic and usually lead to big plays. *Setup plays* are more of a balanced attack.

Reminder: The *line of scrimmage* is the starting point for each play an offensive team initiates; it is also the starting point for certain special teams plays—for example: the punt team, field-goal team, and extra-point team will each start or initiate their action from the *line of scrimmage*.

Football is a game about *gaining territory* as much as it is about scoring points. Repeatedly, a team gains territory to advance the football down the field. Essentially, you gain territory in order to get points. **Moving the sticks** is a necessary progression for securing 1st downs and 1st & 10s.

Moving the sticks signifies each successful attempt at *gaining territory*—each time a team gets a 1st down or 1st & 10, the yard markers move (i.e., the sticks move); a new series of downs begins, and the next attempt for a 1st down or 1st & 10 starts all over again. *Moving the sticks* is the progress a team makes on all successful scoring drives.

Over and over again in every American football game, there will be multiple plays where the difference in a 1st down or a touchdown is determined by inches. For that reason, American football is often referred to as a *game of inches*.

In American football, every sequence, down, and play has a winner and a loser.

Remember: It's an offensive team's strategy to have a *balanced attack* (balance in both the running game and passing game) in order to keep the defensive team off-balance. When an offensive team has good execution in both the running game and the passing game, the strategy for a balanced attack is successful.

However, keep in mind that it's the defensive team's strategy to make the opponents' offensive team one-dimensional. This occurs when the defensive team dominates their opponents' offensive team in one particular phase of the game—for example, when they shut down the running game or the passing game, thereby forcing the opponent to rely on only one phase of the game, instead of having both options.

There are a number of ways a football team can **stop the game clock**. A team can *stop the game clock* by running **out of bounds** (the area on the football field outside of the field of play—identified by thick white lines on the side of the field and white lines around the end-zone area) with the football, by throwing an *incomplete pass* (when a receiver [WR] does not catch a pass thrown to him, or when the quarterback [QB] throws an inaccurate pass that does not get to the intended receiver), by throwing the football *out of bounds*, or by calling a timeout. Each team gets three timeouts per half. Note: Unused timeouts do not carry over to the next half. If a team only uses one of their three timeouts in the first half, they lose the other two timeouts. When the second half starts, the team will have three new timeouts. The game clock also stops toward the end of each half when there are two minutes remaining on the game clock; this occurs at the end of the second quarter and the end of the fourth quarter. This stoppage is called the **two-minute warning** because it is the last two-minutes of each half.

There are different strategies that come into play during the *two-minute warning*. First, if a team has a lead as halftime is approaching and their offensive team has possession of the football, they will go into what's called the **two-minute offense** (an offense specifically designed to score quickly in the last two minutes of a half—also called a ***"hurry-up" offense***); there is a sense of urgency in the last two minutes to try to score and extend the lead. Second, the opposite is true, if a team is trailing on the scoreboard, and their offensive team has possession of the football in the last two minutes of the first half, there is a sense of urgency to try to score in order to reduce the lead. Remember, when the team that's winning is in their *two-minute offense* before halftime, in most cases, their objective is to score to *increase* their lead. Conversely, when a team is losing and they are in their *two-minute offense*, in most cases, their objective is to score in order to *reduce* the lead.

The strategy tends to change regarding the last two minutes of the second half. When a team is in the lead, most teams will try to avoid any mistakes that will allow their opponents an opportunity to make a comeback. In addition, most teams in this scenario will also try to run the game clock out, eliminating any chance for their opponents to get the football back.

Another strategy in this situation revolves around the idea that there are many teams that will try to get as many 1st downs (gain as much territory) as possible while running the game clock down, and if necessary, they will *punt* the football (give up possession of the football by kicking, usually on 4th down) to their opponent with the strategy to create a really long distance for the opponents' offensive team to have to cover before they can attempt to score—all with a limited amount of time left on the game clock. This makes the probability of the opposing team's comeback less likely.

An additional strategy is when a team is trailing in the last two minutes of the second half. The strategy that's most commonly used is when the offensive team will go into their *two-minute offense* and attempt to throw passes toward the sidelines so that the wide receivers (WRs) can try to get out of bounds after they catch the football in order to stop the game clock; this would help preserve time in their comeback attempt. In addition, some teams will occasionally throw a pass deep in the middle of the field, knowing that the opponents are aware of the fact that they would like to throw passes toward the sidelines in order to get out of bounds and stop the game clock. So, in some instances, the defensive team will shift their defense and position more players near the sidelines. As a result, this opens up the middle of the football field for the offensive team to take advantage for a big play because of the open zones or areas.

Often in these circumstances, the offensive team tends to be the aggressor and many defensive teams use a passive strategy called **prevent defense**. The focus of the *prevent defense* is to prevent the offensive team from scoring in the last two minutes of the first half or the last two minutes of the second half. However, because this strategy is so conservative and so passive, it usually allows the offensive team to make large gains in territory—and usually very quickly, much to the advantage of the offensive team. In one way, the *prevent defense* defies conventional wisdom in that it accelerates the offensive team's comeback attempt.

Again, there are **Four Key Indicators for Success for an Offensive Team**:

1. *3rd down conversions*: This refers to the number of times an offensive team is successful on their 3rd-down attempts in securing a 1st down or 1st & 10. For instance, if an offensive team has twelve 3rd-down attempts over the course of the entire game, and they secure five 1st & 10s on those 3rd-down attempts, then the offensive team would be 5 of 12 on 3rd-down conversions.

2. *Turnover ratio*: Each team's strategy requires the offensive team to *protect* the football (not turn it over or lose it to the opponents' defensive team). It's a strategy for the defensive team to *force turnovers* (create turnovers or take away the football from the opponents' offensive team). The number of times a team turns the football over to the other team, compared to the number of times they force their opponents to turn over the football, or they take away the football from their opponents, is the *turnover ratio*. For example, if the home team finishes the game with 1 turnover and the visiting team finishes the game with 3 turnovers, the home team would win the turnover battle or turnover ratio, 3 to 1, for this game. In most cases, the team that wins the *turnover ratio* will win the game. Especially in the case when the turnover ratio is drastically different, the team with a significantly higher number of turnovers will usually lose the game. There's a saying in American football—"Turnovers kill." This saying holds up because turnovers "kill" opportunities for the offensive team's attempts to score. They kill the offensive team's chances of outscoring their opponents. This ultimately reduces the team's chances of winning the game.

3. *Red zone success*: All football teams emphasize the importance of having *red zone success*. The red zone is the location on the foot-

ball field that stretches from the 20-yard line to the end zone. A strategy to have red zone success is paramount for each team because the red zone is the best scoring position on the football field. There is a direct correlation with winning teams and red zone success. For example, if a football team is 5-1, meaning they have 5 wins and 1 loss, odds are that their winning record, in part, is attributed to their red zone success.

4. Time of possession: The total amount of time a football team has the football is *time of possession*. When a team has the football on any scoring drive, time of possession is determined by the time they start their scoring drive to the time they actually score. For example, if an offensive team took possession of the football in the second quarter with 7:30 on the game clock, and they have an eight-play scoring drive that ends with 3:30 left on the game clock, *time of possession* for this scoring drive is 4 minutes. To determine the **total time of possession**, you add the time of possession for every possession the offensive team has over the course of the entire game. As a strategy, football teams would like to win the time of possession battle.

To be successful, football teams have to find *different ways to win*. Some wins may come from the strength and success of the strategy and execution of the defensive team; and for other games, the wins may come from the strength and success of the strategy and execution of the offensive team or the special teams.

Again, relationship teams are comparable in that, to be successful, like football teams, relationship teams have to find *different ways to win* (or to be successful). Relationship teams may have success based on the strength of a specific strategy one month or two months, maybe even for a year or five years. But it may be necessary to find a *different way to win* in the subsequent months or years to follow.

When you envision the image of all three teams (offensive team, defensive team, and special teams) working in unity, the picture is a collage of talents, personalities, and alliances. The ability to frame the right strategy and find different ways to win is a necessary strategy for football teams on all levels—little-league football, middle-school football, high-school football, college football, and especially for NFL teams.

CHAPTER 8

Execution

Qualitative Component

*T*he **execution** is the final act of a mental motion picture, which results from numerous takes—both mental and physical—concerning previews of an anticipated and expected scene. **Sticking to the script** is a major part in a team's game day *execution*.

Execution is to a football team what *quality time* is to a relationship team. The quality time for a relationship team is certainly more important for all of the members involved than the quantity of time. *Execution* is the qualitative component for a football team. The quality of the *execution* of plays is more important than the quantity of plays.

At different levels of the game, to varying degrees, coaches practice, organize, and script out a *game plan* before each game. This *game plan* is the blueprint of how a coach plans to handle every situation and scenario he anticipates and expects to happen over the course of a game. Some coaches specifically script the first 10, 15, or 20 offensive plays of a game, which they plan to execute regardless of what their opponents do with their defensive plays.

The head coach, offensive coordinator, defensive coordinator, and special teams coach use laminated sheets full of plays as their game day scripts. Players on the offensive team, defensive team and special teams practice on how they will execute against these different situations when they use *situational preparation*, (remember, this is when a team uses planning and preparing for different situations by studying the opponents' personnel and tendencies). Players are coached on how important it is to *stick to the script* with regards to good *execution*.

Audibles are necessary adjustments made by means of verbal communication, hand signals, or eye signals. These adjustments are necessary when a quarterback (QB) or defensive captain realizes that the play and/or *formation* (the way the offensive team or the defensive team lines up to execute a play) called in the huddle is a total mismatch against the opponents' line-up. In order to avert a really bad play or a potential catastrophe, teams have a certain number of calls or plays already prepared for use as an adjustment in these kind of scenarios. These prescripted and preplanned adjustments are called *audibles*.

Similar to the case with football teams, adjustments on the move (*audibles*) are extremely important during challenging situations for relationship teams. The ability to avert any major setback is crucial in the end game for both football teams and relationship teams. If a relationship team planned to upgrade an automobile this year, yet their financial condition took a hit, as a result of a couple of unexpected medical expenditures, then the adjustment (*audible*, for the relationship team) would be to put off upgrading the automobile until the next year.

Some teams use the *running game* to open up the *passing game*, and other teams use the *passing game* to open up the *running game*. They use the phase of the game that is their strength to develop a **rhythm** in the game. A lot of offensive teams like to develop a *rhythm* and control the **pace** of the game. (Here again there is a comparison with relationship teams, when one member or the other tries to control the *rhythm* and *pace* of the relationship team.) Generally speaking, *rhythm* and *pace* are more important for an offensive team than the defensive team. Defensive teams will occasionally use certain tactics, such as a **blitz** (a type of defensive pressure where the defensive team rushes more men than the offensive team has the capacity to block on a given play), in order to disrupt the offensive team's *rhythm* and *pace* and make a big defensive stop or create a turnover.

Having **possession** of the football means to be in control or holding the football. To be in *possession* is an advantage for the offensive team, primarily because it gives them an opportunity to score. Having *possession* of the football also gives the offensive team an opportunity to manage or utilize the game clock to their advantage. In addition, *possession* of the football also means that the offensive team is on the path to *gain territory*.

Field position is enormously important in American football because it is linked to the odds of succeeding. It's a great indicator of a team's chances of scoring. It is difficult for an offensive team to be successful when they start most of their possessions with bad *field positions*. The more frequently a football team gets good *field position*, the more likely they will have success in executing scoring opportunities. Good *field* *position* is a key in getting into the end zone. The more frequently a team gets to the end zone, the more their success is guaranteed.

Let's recap: When a team loses possession of the football to their opponents by means of a fumble or an interception, they commit what's called a *turnover*. This means that the offensive team will have one less opportunity to move or drive the football in an attempt to gain territory. It also means one less possibility for a score, and it gives their opponents' offensive team one more opportunity to score.

Defensive teams refer to securing a *turnover* as a **takeaway**. At the end of the game, the team that secures more turnovers than their opponents wins what is referred to as the *turnover battle*. Every possession a team has is important, because each one represents a scoring opportunity.

Change of possession happens most frequently on 4th down, when an offensive team does not get a 1st and 10 (when an offensive team fails on their 1st down, 2nd down, and 3rd down attempts to gain 10 yards) and elects to change possession via a punt on 4th down. *Change of possession* also happens when a team elects to attempt a 4th down play and fails. *Change of possession* will also occur when a team commits a turnover or after a team scores. The two least-desired means of a change of possession are a turnover and a failed attempt on a 4th down play.

Remember the eight times *change of possession* occurs:

1. On 4th down, when an offensive team elects to punt the football after their unsuccessful attempts to gain a total of 10 yards on 1st down, 2nd down, and 3rd down.
2. When an offensive team chooses to execute a 4th down play and is unsuccessful.
3. When an offensive team commits a turnover.
4. After a defensive team commits a turnover.
5. After a special teams commits a turnover.
6. After an offensive team scores.
7. After a special teams scores.
8. After a defensive team scores.

Sudden change is when unexpected things happen that bring about a hasty transition. One moment, the offensive team is on the football field, and then, as a result of a turnover, the defensive team has to rush out onto the football field. The bottom line here is, stuff happens. *Sudden change* is most recognized in American football in the form of a turnover. This situation is usually caused either by a fumble or an interception. *Sudden change* requires not only that a team make adjustments but also that they make adjustments on the run or on the move. Oftentimes, not making these adjustments leads to major setbacks, and sometimes even failed outcomes—translation: losses.

Time of possession is the total time an offensive team possesses the football on any given drive. It's also the total amount of time an offensive team possesses the football for the entire game. *Time of possession* is applicable to the number of plays or the number of opportunities an offensive team has, in which they can try to score. In most cases, when a team possesses the football longer, it also means they had more offensive plays. When an offensive team wins the time of possession battle, it's safe to conclude that this offensive team has had more opportunities to gain territory on the field and more opportunities to score over the course of the football game.

There are different **zones** on the football field. Keep in mind that the playing field in American football is **120 yards** in length and 100 yards from one **end zone** (the location or *zone* on the football field in which one of the teams can score a *touchdown* [TD] or a *safety*) to the other *end zone*. Both *end zones* are 10 yards in length from the beginning of the end zone to the back of the end zone. In short, the *end zone* is a scoring zone and a celebration zone.

The 50-yard line divides the 100-yard playing field. This is the middle of the football field and is called **midfield**. Also keep in mind, the middle of the field—*midfield*—separates one team's end of the football field from their opponents' end of the football field. When an offensive team is on their own end of the field, they are on the side of *midfield* that is farthest away from their opponents' end zone, which is the end zone they are trying to get to in order to score.

Note: You will only see one 50-yard line on the football field. However, you will see a 40-yard line, a 30-yard line, a 20-yard line, and a 10-yard line on both sides of *midfield*. And, there is a *goal line* on both sides of *midfield*, which is the beginning of each end zone.

Let's look at a couple of examples to understand an offensive team's starting location or *zone* on the football field when they start a possession. First, if an offensive team starts their possession on the 15-yard line in the **black zone** (the zone that is farthest away from the end zone where the offensive team needs to get to in order to score), it means that they have to drive or move the football 85 yards to score a touchdown (TD). They are starting their possession on their own end of the football field, and they are striving to gain territory with 1st downs.

Another example: Let's say a team receives a *punt* (when the opponents elect to kick the football on 4th down as a result of their failing to secure a 1st & 10—i.e., 10 yards—on their 1st down, 2nd down, and 3rd down attempts), and the opponents' punt-returner catches the football on their own 20-yard line and returns the football for 20 yards. The opponents' offensive team, in this case, will start their possession on their own 40-yard line, which is considered good field position because the closer an offensive team is to *midfield* (away from the *black zone*), the more they are considered to have good field position. This is the 40-yard line that is farthest away from the end zone they are trying to get to in order to score. They have 60 yards to go in order to score a touchdown (TD). In this example, the offensive team is starting their possession in the **gray zone**.

Let's take a closer look at the different zones on an American football field. The *black zone* is when a team takes possession of the football anywhere between their own goal line and their own 20-yard line. Remember: This is the distance that is farthest away from their opponents' goal line or end zone (the end zone they need to get to in order to score a touchdown [TD]). The *black zone* is considered the most dangerous area of the football field for an offensive team, and it is considered extremely dangerous if the offensive team starts their possession on the 10-yard line (or less) in the *black zone*. It's important to note: Any mistake in this area of the field—a fumble or an interception—usually proves to be costly for an offensive team. Often, when an offensive team commits a turnover in the *black zone*, either the defensive team turns it into a defensive score, or they put their offensive team in great field position to score a touchdown (TD) or a field goal (FG).

Let me give you an example of how it can be dangerous for an offensive team to start their possession on their own 15-yard line—the *black zone*. On their very first play, the offensive team *fumbles* the football (loses possession of the football by dropping it on the field) and the defensive team *recovers* it (secures possession of the football) on the 15-yard line. The defensive team will give their offensive team possession of the football on their opponents' 15-yard line. This means that their offensive team would be starting their possession in the *red zone* (the distance from the opponents' 20-yard line to the opponents' goal line). The offensive team only needs 15 yards to score a touchdown (TD).

The **gray zone** is the location or zone on the football field from the 21-yard line on one side of midfield to the 21-yard line on the other side of the football field. The *gray zone* is the zone on the field where the offensive team has less pressure than they face in the *black zone* and the *red zone*. For instance, in the *black zone*, it's very critical for an offensive team not to make any mistakes that would give the opponent an advantage with regards to scoring. On the other hand, in the *red zone*, it is critical for an offensive team to secure some type of score—either a touchdown (TD) or a field goal (FG)—because it is challenging for offensive teams to get to the *red zone* with high regularity. So, the higher the percentage of success an offensive team has in the red zone with regards to scoring points, the higher the percentage of success a team will have with regards to winning.

The **red zone** is the location or zone on the football field from the opponents' 20-yard line to the opponents' goal line. It's the 20-yard line nearest the end zone that an offensive team needs to get to in order to score a touchdown (TD). This is the hot spot on the football field for an offensive team, in regards to scoring. The *red zone* is generally considered the part of the football field where the chances of scoring are statistically higher than any other location or zone on the field. Generally speaking, unless an offensive team commits a turnover (when the offensive team gives up possession of the football to the defensive team by either a fumble or an interception), they generally will secure a score in the *red zone*. Even if the offensive team doesn't score a touchdown (TD), they will at least score with a field goal (FG). It extremely important for an offensive team not to make any mistakes in the red zone and to secure some points because it's a challenge to get to the *red zone* with a high level of frequency.

The **end zone** is the 10 yards that begins at the opponents' goal line and stretches to the end of the field. This is the 10-yard zone that each offensive team is striving to get to every time they get possession of the football. This is the area or zone on the football field where a touchdown (TD) or safety is scored. In short, the *end zone* is the end game.

Regarding the different zones on the football field, remember:

- The *black zone* is from the goal line to the 20-yard line on the offensive team's end of the field. Again, this is the 20-yard line that is farthest away from the end zone that an offensive team needs to get to in order to score a touchdown (TD).
- The *gray zone* is from the 21-yard line on one side of the football field to 21-yard line on the other side of the football field.
- The *red zone* is from the opponents' 20-yard line to the opponents' goal line—the 20-yard line nearest the opponents' end zone.
- The *end zone* is a 10-yard zone that begins at the opponents' goal line and stretches to the end of the field. This is the scoring zone.

Note: When you are looking at the football field, the *gray zone* stays the same for either offensive team; however, the *black zone* for one offensive team is actually the *red zone* for the opponents' offensive team, and vice versa.

It's interesting how zones on the football field can be viewed as similar to zones in relationships. Relationship teams that spend a lot of time in the *black zone*, similar to the football field, are in the zone that is farthest away from the scoring zone. The black zone for relationship teams is like bad field position; it's the zone that's very dangerous; any mistake can prove to be costly to the success of the relationship team.

The *gray zone* for a relationship team is not really good field position, but neither is it really bad field position. This is the area for a relationship team that probably feels like status quo. This is a zone for a relationship team where mistakes, errors, and misfortunes tend to be less critical than they are in the black zone. This is the zone where relationship teams have to stay focused in order to keep things moving in a positive direction—striving to move into the red zone.

The *red zone* for a relationship team is similar to great field position for a football team. This is the hot zone on a football field, and this is the zone for a relationship team where the chances of scoring are statistically higher than they are in the black zone and the gray zone. This is the zone where relationship teams put themselves in position to have success year after year, season after season.

The end zone is where a relationship team celebrates their victories and successes. This is the celebration zone.

The different zones on the football field affect a football team's execution. There is a clear correlation to the effectiveness and efficiency of an offensive team's execution when you analyze it from the standpoint of possession of the football in the black zone, gray zone, and red zone, respectively.

When players get caught up in the emotions of the game, they have to stay focused and manage their emotions so that they can consistently execute at a high level. It is very difficult for a player to execute when their emotions are out of control.

Men, in general, are stereotypically defined as non-emotional. And this argument is generally highlighted in terms of relationships. I reiterate *stereotypically*—Take, for example, a quote-unquote non-emotional man in a relationship. If this same man is a football fan, I would venture to say that if he is observed closely on game day, chances are, whether his football team wins or loses, he will probably display a lot of emotions during the course of the football game. Men are certainly more emotional than the stereotype would lead you to believe. In many instances, women are criticized far too often in terms of being too emotional in relationships. And they are criticized not only for being too emotional but for being too emotional compared to men. In all fairness, if men are allowed their autonomy with respect to their emotions of the game in American football, perhaps women should be allowed to have the same autonomy with regards to their emotions in the game of love.

When I played in the NFL, there were three aspects of a game where my emotions ran the highest. One was during the national anthem. I always loved hearing the national anthem so much because I'm very proud to be an American. And I was always proud to represent the team I was playing for, as well as the city. To this day, I still love hearing the national anthem being played before a game.

My emotions also always ran high when the song "We Will Rock You" was blasted on the stadium speakers. This was usually during a time when the crowd was fired up and looking for the defense to make a great play—either to preserve a lead or get the football back for our offensive team. As a player, during this stage of the game, when the beat of this song was booming throughout the stadium, I could feel a liquid aggression running through my veins. I was definitely ready to knock somebody off his feet. We had a very mean defensive team that was always ready to rock the opposing offensive team's world.

Finally, my emotions ran high when the crowd noise was off the charts. The energy of the fans definitely had a confluence with the energy of the defensive team. When I was a starter as a defensive cornerback with the New Orleans Saints, our defensive team gave the Saints' fans much to cheer about on a regular basis. The Saints' defensive team routinely performed at a very high level. And in return, the Saints' fans provided us with crowd noise that was incredible and very loud. The crowd noise was so incredible that it gave our defensive team an emotional edge and a surge of energy. After every home game in the Superdome, many of my teammates and I would joke about the headaches we had at the end of the games as a result of the crowd noise.

In an American football game, both players and coaches alike consistently face the challenge of *out-of-control emotions*. There was one instance when the head coach and I faced out-of-control emotions in a playoffs game with the Saints. Two games prior to this playoffs game, I had suffered a serious shoulder injury—a second-degree shoulder separation. As a result of my injury, I took a pain-killer shot in my shoulder in order to play in this playoffs game. After the shot, my shoulder was patched up, padded up, and wrapped up. Due to this special wrapping and padding, I had extremely limited mobility with my right shoulder and arm on the side of the shoulder separation.

During the course of the game, a pass was thrown to the opposing receiver (WR) in the end zone on my side of the field. I was in a position where I needed to extend my right shoulder, arm, and hand to defend a pass. Even though I was in the proper position, I could not defend the pass as a result of the injury, padding, wrap, and limited mobility. As a result, the receiver caught a pass for a touchdown. I jogged off the field in frustration from not being able to execute the defensive play the way I normally would have. To further exacerbate the issue, as I approached the sidelines and headed to the bench, my coach had a temporary mental lapse. Clearly, he had forgotten about the fact that I had taken a shot and was patched up, padded up, and wrapped up, with a second-degree shoulder separation. He lost control of his emotions and commenced to yell and swear at me. And he asked why I hadn't made a play on the football. Of course, I'm sure the question stemmed from the fact that it was a play that I would normally make because I was a very disciplined and efficient pass defender. And the irony in the situation was that I was a *no excuse* player. However, this was not a normal scenario, with the seriousness of the injury and the limited mobility.

So, with the shock of my coach yelling and swearing at me, when in fact, I had put everything on the line and represented my team—though I was playing at far less than 60% health and playing at a major disadvantage—in the heat of the moment, my emotions got the best of me, and I responded in kind. I yelled back at the coach and asked him if he had forgotten that I was playing with a freakin' patched up, padded up, wrapped up, second-degree separated shoulder, and it was freakin' simply not possible for me to lift my freakin' arm and hand to make a play on the freakin' football. At this time, my mentor—the late great linebacker Sam Mills grabbed me and escorted me to the bench; he talked to me and calmed me down.

In the heat of the battle, players and coaches have to deal with *out-of-control emotions*. At the end of the day, what's ultimately important is that calmer heads do prevail.

Emotions of the game don't stop on the football field. There are so
many players that have a very difficult time executing the **transition** from
the game. This consequently is a result of the passion and deep love for the
game. I speak from experience—it took me five years to get adjusted—to
transition from the game. By *adjusted*, I mean able to accept the fact that
my NFL career was over and it was time to do something different with my
life—sooner than I had hoped or planned. This harsh reality is indeed a
bitter pill to swallow. Nevertheless, even with finally accepting the *transition* from the game, year after year, for the last seven years, I've tried to
find ways to get reconnected to the NFL. I've attempted to secure positions
as an assistant coach, quality-control coach, and director of player
development—all to no avail. My biggest pursuit now with regards to
being connected with the NFL and to satisfy my passion for the game is to
secure an opportunity as a professional football (NFL) analyst with one of
the networks. I love American football—in particular, professional football
(National Football League), and I would relish the opportunity to observe
and analyze professional football games on-air for many years to come.

But to get back to the subject at hand, *emotions of the game* are
very real—it's incumbent upon both players and coaches to control their
emotions to the extent that they can execute effectively and efficiently on
every play. Both players and coaches have to be able to execute with their
emotions running high. During the course of an American football game,
players, coaches, and fans take an emotional roller-coaster ride.

When it comes to execution, **key plays** trump statistics. A team may
outrank another team statistically in a number of categories, but on game
day, the underdog still has a chance to win the game by simply making
more *key plays*, making fewer mistakes, and having better execution than
the team with all of the high statistical rankings. Being *good on paper* does
not guarantee wins and does not guarantee that a team is going to give a
good performance. Being **good on paper** is a term used for a team with
more talent, but again, being *good on paper* doesn't translate into wins. It's
all about execution.

This is also true of **hype**. Some teams, because of certain a star player
or because of the number of star players they have on their team, may get
all of the *hype* before a game. *Hype* comes from media coverage as well as
from the rave reviews of football analysts prior to a game. However, the
hype and expectation from the media and the football analysts has never
won a football game. After all, expectations are not synonymous with

execution. Neither can expectations produce execution. Ultimately, both players and coaches have to execute on each and every play of every game.

There are many people who debate whether **momentum** in an American football game is real or not. I believe *momentum* is real. I think *momentum* is the confluence of the positive energy of the players and the positive energy of the fans inside of a stadium. The confluence of the two energies forms an imaginary wave against the opponents, and that confluence has an impact on them. In some instances, the opponents' efforts and attempts seem to hit this imaginary wave of *momentum*, sinking their execution. And in other instances, the team with the momentum on their side seems to ride on this imaginary wave, succeeding in their execution of key plays, which results in scoring.

Momentum notwithstanding, a team's success in an American football game comes from a simple but challenging act: Execution. Execution. Execution.

CHAPTER 9

Scoring

Quantitative Component

*T*here is nothing that adds drama and suspense to a football game like **scoring**. There simply isn't anything that rivals putting points up on the scoreboard. Big hits are intense and breathtaking, but *scoring* produces drama and anticipation.

Perhaps the opponents' offensive team is one of the best in the league—fans of the home team ask themselves, "Can our defensive team match up against them?" Or they question whether their offensive team will have to play a perfect game in order to stay in the game and have any chance at winning. Another scenario: The fans know their own offensive team is pretty good, but the opponents' defensive team is great—in fact, they are the #1 defensive team in the entire league. Maybe they question whether their offensive team can even score a touchdown against the opposing team.

Every team has a **strategy** for their offensive team, defensive team, and special teams. Even though a team may have one unit that is stronger than the other two units, it always takes a combined effort from all three units—in trying to score as well as in trying to stop their opponents from *scoring*—in order to win a game. Football teams are always more successful when they get contributions from all three teams: *offensive team, defensive team*, and *special teams*.

Typically, the *offensive team* is expected to do most of the scoring. Some teams are lucky because their offensive team is basically a "scoring machine." The offensive team is also expected to make as few mistakes as possible, so as to not put the defensive team at any major disadvantage.

The *defensive team* is generally expected to hold the opponents' offensive team to as few points as possible—preferably less than the amount of points their own offensive team puts up on the scoreboard. In the past, the general consensus in the NFL was that if a defensive team kept their opponents' offensive team to less than 17 points, they should win the game. In addition, anytime a defensive team scores, it is a huge bonus.

The *special teams*—punt team, punt-return team, kickoff team, and kickoff-return team—are each depended upon for field positioning and for stopping the opponents' punt-return team and kickoff-return team from putting the opponents' offensive team in good field position. Note: The *punt team* defends the opposing *punt-return team*; and the *kickoff team* defends the opposing *kickoff-return team*. It's a major plus when the punt-return team or the kickoff-return team returns a punt or a kickoff, respectively, for a *touchdown* (TD).

The star players do a lot of the scoring on American football teams because it's expected of them. However, with the large number of role players on each team, *scoring* contributions come from multiple players. For example, keep in mind that the kicker (K) generally gets a lot of attempts at scoring. When the kicker (K) is efficient, he scores points in both *field goals* (FGs) and *extra points* (PATs). Some role players solidify their significance on the team with their skill for scoring.

Scoring also creates **uncertainty and anticipation**. Is the home team's score enough? Does a particular score bring the team close enough to have a chance to win (because the home team is losing)? If a home team is winning, does a certain score give the home team a big enough lead to hold on and win the game?

Not the players, coaches, nor fans have any definitive insight on the actual outcome of a game before it is played. The *uncertainty of the outcome* is something that players, coaches, and fans alike all have to deal with going into each game. What no one knows during the triumph of tailgating and during the teams' pregame warm-ups is which team will be victorious at the end of the day. Even though the players, coaches, and fans go into each game with the *uncertainty of the outcome*, they all go into each game with the anticipation that their team will perform well, and that there will be plenty of plays to cheer and celebrate. *Uncertainty and anticipation* creates an emotional roller-coaster ride—for players, coaches, and fans; these emotions are the underpinning of excitement and energy in every stadium before and during the course of an American football game.

There are four different quantities of scores in American football that register on the scoreboard:

- "1 point" (Referred to as an *"extra point"* or *"point-after-touch-down*—**PAT**," this is an offensive score.)
- "2 points" (Referred to as a *"two-point conversion*," this is an offensive score.)
- "2 points" (Referred to as a *"safety*," this is a defensive score.)
- "3 points" (Referred to as a *"field goal*—**FG**," this is an offensive score.)
- "6 points" (Referred to as a *"touchdown*—**TD**," this can be an offensive score or a defensive score.)

There are four ways for an offensive team to score points in an American football game. A *touchdown* (TD), which is worth six (6) points, is the most treasured score over the course of a game because it accelerates the overall aim to secure enough points to win the game. In order to score a *touchdown* (TD), a team must carry the football into the opponents' end zone or catch the football in the opponents' end zone. The two means of scoring a *touchdown* (TD) come from either the running game or the passing game.

After each touchdown (TD), a team has the option to kick an *extra point* (PAT) or run a play for a *two-point conversion*. A team scores one (1) point when the football is successfully kicked through (between) the opponents' goal posts after a touchdown (TD). A team scores two (2) points when, after a touchdown (TD), the football is carried into the opponents' end zone or a pass is caught in the opponents' end zone.

In most cases, teams will kick for the *extra point*; one exception is when a team is trailing on the scoreboard, and they need a *two-point conversion* in order to make a comeback. Another instance in which a team will strategically go for a *two-point conversion* is when they come from behind— they've scored a touchdown (TD), and they now have a one-point lead. So they will use the *two-point conversion* to create a three-point lead, making sure the opponents can only tie the game in the event that the opposing offensive team might get into a scoring position for a *field goal* attempt before the game ends.

An additional way for the offensive team to score is a *field goal* (FG). A team scores three (3) points when they successfully kick the football through (between) the opponents' goal posts. A *field goal* (FG) is generally kicked when a team does not secure a 1st & 10 and, on 4th down, they are confident that they are within striking distance to secure a score by kicking a *field goal* (FG). (Reminder: To secure a 1st & 10 means to gain a total of 10 yards on the combined down attempts, thereby securing the opportunity to move on to the next series of downs.) Never confuse a *field goal* (FG) with an *extra point* (PAT). **Keep in mind:** An *extra point* (PAT) is only kicked after a team scores a *touchdown* (TD); hence, it is an *extra point* (PAT).

Remember, there are four ways for an *offensive team* to score points:

- *touchdown* (TD)—worth six (6)
- *extra point* (PAT)—worth one (1)
- *two-point conversion*—worth two (2)
- *field goal* (FG)—worth three (3).

Offensive teams use both their **running game** (the quarterback [QB] handing the football to a running back [RB] for a running play) and **passing game** (the quarterback throwing the football to a receiver who catches the football for a passing play) strategically to try to score against their opponents' defensive team. Some teams' strength is the running game; other teams' is the passing game; there are also a few teams who are fortunate enough to be strong in both the running game and the passing game.

This dual strength is referred to as having a **balanced attack**, which simply means that the offensive team has an advantage in that they can challenge their opponents' defensive team with both the *running game* and the *passing game*. And because they have a *balanced attack,* they have the capacity to score equally as much with either the *running game* or the *passing game*.

Remember, a key strategy for a defensive team is to make their opponents' offensive team *one-dimensional,* (which means that they shut down either the offensive team's running game or passing game), forcing the offensive team to only have one option to use in their effort to score. So when the defensive team shuts down the offensive team's running game, for example, the offensive team is forced to focus only on their passing game, and the defensive team, in turn, is aware of this and is even more prepared to defend the passing game. This is, without a doubt, an advantage for the defensive team.

There are four ways for a defensive team to score points in an American football game: a **safety**, which is worth two (2) points, an **interception return, fumble return**, and **field goal block return**, each worth six (6) points.

A *safety* is when a defensive player tackles an offensive player in his own end zone (this is the black zone area). An *interception return* is when a quarterback throws a pass that's intended for a receiver, but it is intercepted or picked-off by a defensive player and returned for a touchdown (pick-6). A *fumble return* is when an offensive player accidently loses possession, drops or has the football intentionally knocked out of his possession, and a defensive player recovers it and returns the fumble recovery for a touchdown. A *field goal block return* is when the offensive team attempts a field goal and the defensive team blocks it, and then returns the block for a touchdown.

Remember, there are four ways for a *defensive team* to score point:

- *Safety*—worth two (2)
- *Interception return*—worth six (6)
- *Fumble return*—worth six (6)
- *Field goal return*—worth six (6)

Offensive Scoring

The 2011 NFL season opened with an explosive performance by the two previous Super Bowl winners. The New Orleans Saints (Super Bowl XLIV Champions) face off against the Green Bay Packers (the league's defending Super Bowl XLV champions). A perfectly scheduled match-up to start the season, the Packers were fortunate to be hosting in front of a sellout crowd of 70,555 at Lambeau Field, in Green Bay, Wisconsin, as opposed to the alternative—having to face this challenging opponent in the Mercedes-Benz Superdome in New Orleans, Louisiana, which could have yielded a different result.

This game featured a lot of scoring and very little defense, which was evidence of how good both of these offensive teams were. The New Orleans Saints' offensive team had 477 total yards against the Green Bay Packers' defensive team. And the Packers' offensive team took that up another notch over the Saints' defensive team, with 399 total yards on offense. Both teams combined for 876 total yards on offense, making both defensive teams appear nonexistent.

In this high-scoring shootout, the New Orleans Saints had four touchdowns (TDs), four extra points (PATs), and two field goals (FGs); one of the four touchdowns (TD) scored was on special teams—a punt-return for a 72-yard touchdown (TD). The Green Bay Packers had six touchdowns (TDs) and six extra points (PATs); one of the touchdowns scored was on special teams—a kickoff-return for a 108-yard touchdown (TD). The Packers prevailed in this high-scoring season opener, 42 to 34, with both teams combining for ten touchdowns (TDs), ten extra points (PATs), two field goals (FG) and 76 total points.

Even though players, coaches, and fans each have their own unique way of celebrating, one thing is sure—after every big play, every defensive stand, and each score, each of them celebrate together. There's screaming, yelling, shouting, clapping, high-fives, hugs, blowing kisses at the fans, bowing to the fans, chest pumping, etc. There are many unique and colorful ways in which players, coaches, and fans celebrate scoring.

Over the history of the NFL, there have been many players who have distinguished themselves with their unique **celebrations** after scoring. For example, there have been dancing, taking off helmets to show their faces, chest pumping, throwing the football in the stands to a fan, eating a fan's box of popcorn, taking a cheerleader's pom-poms, and even making a call from a mobile phone in the end zone. Individual *celebrations* are intriguing; however, I think group or team *celebrations* are more captivating. There are several notable team *celebrations*; the Washington Redskins had the *Fun Bunch* celebration; the Denver Broncos had the *Mile High Salute*; the St. Louis Rams, the *Bob-n-Weave*; and the Green Bay Packers, the *Lambeau Leap*.

It would be really cool to see each team in the NFL come up with a celebration that reflects and represents their own team and city. However, it's not so cool when other players and other teams do their version of the Lambeau Leap. This is a celebration that originated with the Green Bay Packers at Lambeau Field in

Green Bay, Wisconsin. The NFL should allow each team to have their own unique celebration without the fear of being penalized for celebrating. If the Green Bay Packers can celebrate their scoring with their fans without concern of being penalized, each and every team in the National Football League should be allowed to have a *scoring celebration* that is unique to their team and city.

Special Teams Scoring

Note: If a kickoff return is fumbled and recovered by the defending team, it can be returned for a touchdown (TD).

Note: If a punt return is fumbled and recovered by the defending team, it can be returned for a touchdown (TD).

The all-time leading scorer in NFL history is one of my former teammates with the New Orleans Saints—field-goal kicker Morten Andersen; he's definitely a future Hall of Famer. His nickname is "The Great Dane," which is a reference to his Danish roots. Morten has made his mark by scoring 2,544 points in his illustrious career—*field goal* (FG) (.797), *extra points* (PAT)(.988)

Defensive Scoring

There is a defensive score that is stored in the security-deposit box of my memory bank. I remember it like it was yesterday—setting: the Louisiana Superdome in New Orleans. As the sweat drips profusely down my face and from inside my helmet to the top of the AstroTurf® field, I can see the sweat dripping from the faces of my teammates as well, as we conclude our pregame warm-up routine—the foreplay of a football game.

The Superdome is sitting at 72 degrees—no wind, no elements from the weather; a controlled environment with regards to the temperature. Yet the Saints' fans, not so controlled (over 68,000 of them), are worked up and ready. They toss down the aphrodisiac of anticipation, and they are feeling kind of jazzy because it's just about kickoff time. They are ready for their Saints team to go marching in for a victory.

This battle against the Bears is no different than that against any other opponent. You must outscore your opponents in order to win. After all, why else are there more than 68,000 out-of-control, jazzed-up, colorful Saints fans coordinating crowd noises to drive the Chicago Bears into hibernation? These fans, like all American football fans, know that winning is the ultimate goal. They are present to supply the oral energy to fuel scoring because, at the end of the day, scoring is the name of the game.

By late in the fourth quarter, the Chicago Bears are down by 15 points; now you understand what the Saints' fans already comprehend. The Chicago Bears are not mathematically out of the game. They need a touchdown (TD), a two-point conversion, another touchdown (TD), and an extra point (PAT), and then the game will be tied. But the Saints fans are still jazzed up, and there are no signs that the aphrodisiac of anticipation has worn off.

At this instant, a moment in the New Orleans Superdome that I will always remember—before more than 68,000 fans and perhaps millions more watching on television—as the Chicago Bears try to inch closer to our defensive end zone to score, the Bears' quarterback (QB) throws a pass to his receiver (WR) on my side of the field.

I *intercept* the football (when the defensive team catches a pass from the opponents' quarterback [QB], which is intended for one of the opponents' receivers [WRs]) and begin to make my way toward the end zone.

As I return the football, with each stride I make I feel as if the jazzed-up home crowd is in rhythm with my every motion. Every time my feet hit the surface of the field, the crowd and I are in sync. I can feel the vibration of the crowd noise in the Superdome.

Currently, every single one of them is up and on their feet. I refuse to be caught! I run as hard and as fast as I can toward the opponents' end zone. The synergy in the stadium is incredible; every single muscle in my body is refueled by the oral energy of 68,000+ synchronized, screaming fans who know we are reaching the climax they had been anticipating. After a 71-yard interception return, I run into the end zone for a touchdown (TD) (**pick-6**—when a defensive player intercepts or picks off a pass from the quarterback and returns it for a touchdown, it's called a "pick-6.")—a defensive score.

Unanswered points occur when the score is tied, one of the teams scores, and on the subsequent possession(s), the opponents' offensive team does not score any points. It could also refer to a situation when one team is behind on the scoreboard and they score and take the lead, and then the team that previously had the lead does not score any points on their subsequent possession(s). In both cases, these are *unanswered points*.

Here's a closer look at both of these examples; First, let's look at the instance with the score being tied between the teams—one team scores a touchdown (TD) plus the extra point (PAT), and later they score a field goal (FG) for a total of 10 points. This is referred to as scoring 10 *unanswered points*. Now, let's look at the second scenario, when the team that was behind on the scoreboard takes the lead. In this situation, the team scores two touchdowns (TDs), two extra points (PATs), and a field goal (FG). This is referred to as scoring 17 *unanswered points*.

The longer the stretch of the game the team who is behind on the scoreboard goes with unanswered points, the more pressure and more difficult it becomes for this team to make a comeback. It's vital for a team to score and deal with unanswered points; as the game clock ticks away, so do the opportunities for a team to answer unanswered points and make a comeback.

Football fans all over America wear the **Jersey of the Journey** and the **Uniform of Euphoria** every time they step into a stadium to watch an American football game, whether it be little-league football, middle-school football, high-school football, college football, or professional football. Most fans are routinely fixated on the **scoreboard** throughout the course of the game.

Despite the fact that players, coaches, and fans deal with the uncertainty of the outcome and the wave of emotions that streams through football stadiums all over America, the *scoreboard* symbolizes more than just the board where each team registers points—It symbolizes an optical obsession, a pictorial promise, or graphical gratification.

Scoring drive denotes the total number of plays an offensive team executes when they score on any given possession; regardless of whether they score a field goal (FG) or a touchdown (TD), it's a *scoring drive*. Teams that are stronger in the *passing game* tend to score quicker and require fewer plays than teams who focus more on the *running game*.

For example, if an offensive team has a total of 3 running plays and 3 passing plays, and they score a field goal (FG), it is called a 6-play *scoring drive*. Likewise, if an *offensive team* has 8 running plays and 4 passing plays, and it leads to a touchdown (TD), it is called a 12-play *scoring drive*. It's the same when an offensive team throws 2 passes that result in a touchdown (TD) for a score. This is called a 2-play *scoring drive*, even though it's quick and consists of passing plays only.

However, in general, teams with a stronger *running game* not only have longer, sustained *scoring drives*, but they also possess the football longer, allowing their defensive teams to be more rested each time they take the field. The teams with a strong running game also wear down the opponents' defensive team over the course of the game. In addition to possessing the football longer, they decrease the amount of time and opportunities the opponents' offensive team has to score.

Be aware of the fact that long *scoring drives* are successful on two levels. First and foremost, it's always good when an offensive team puts points up on the *scoreboard*. This usually increases the team's odds of winning the game. Secondly, when the offensive team has a long *scoring drive*, they consume a large share of the game clock, which increases their chances of winning the *time of possession battle* (the total amount of time a team possesses the football over the course of a game).

Long, sustained *scoring drives* are especially effective against opponents whose offensive team's strength is the running game because the running game itself normally takes more time off the game clock than does the passing game. Typically, the offensive teams whose strength is the running game are often the offensive teams who are not as efficient in the passing game, which is a quicker method of moving the football. By focusing on long *scoring drives*, the offensive team reduces the amount of time on the game clock and the number of opportunities that the opposing offensive team will have to score.

The team who is leading on the *scoreboard* and who can capitalize on a long *scoring drive* will put their opponents' offensive team in a challenging position. As a result of getting behind and having less time to make a comeback, the opponents' offensive team will be forced to make an adjustment away from their primary strength or the strategy they are most comfortable with (in this example, the running game). Thus, they will spend more time in their passing game, which is the phase of the game in which they are least efficient.

In the event an offensive team is fortunate enough to successfully put together multiple long *scoring drives*, over the course of a game, they could potentially deliver a devastating blow to the opposing defensive team. In the long run, this wears down the opposing defensive team both physically and mentally. The offensive team is usually dominating the game when the opponents' defensive team is on the football field significantly more than the opponents' offensive team. The defensive team becomes weakened physically because of the amount of energy that is exerted unsuccessfully against the opponents' offensive team when they are constantly on the football field with a limited amount of rest. Also, the defensive team is weakened mentally when they become frustrated, because their offensive team is not productive, and their offensive team is constantly losing the time of possession battle.

An exception to this scenario is when an offensive team is so hot that they score quickly and they score often—they are a scoring machine. In this case, it doesn't matter if the defensive team is on the field for a lot of plays because they are winning the game. And amazingly, winning produces energy. So, the defensive team is actually energized in these circumstances.

A *scoring drive* is the total number of times an offensive team's efficiency in execution and effort in gaining territory yields a return on investment in the mode of scoring. The **quantitative component** that can assure a team that they will finish the game victoriously is when a team secures more *scoring drives* than their opponents. Ultimately, when a team outscores their opponents, they win. There is no mystery for this winning equation: Successfully defend your opponents' scoring attempts, avoid unanswered points, and register more points on the *scoreboard* than your opponents. Scoring is not only the name of the game, but it also summarizes the overall outcome of the game.

Score. Score. Score.

Conclusion

*T*his great game of American football, at the end of the day, is paradoxically a love story.

Maybe you're a fan and you love a certain player, a certain coach, or a certain team.

Perhaps you're a die-hard fan and you simply love every facet of the game, especially the confident players, the tenacious players, the role players, the star players, the team players, and maybe even the cocky players or the selfish players. Furthermore, perhaps you have a deep love for the offensive team, the defensive team, or maybe even the special teams. You equally love the sophisticated strategy, the great execution, and the exciting scoring that comes with the game.

By now you know, it doesn't matter if you wear stilettos or loafers; you have as much intrigue and interest as the next follower of the game, and you simply desire to have a great feel for the game because the love that's evolving for the game is real. You have fallen for the game.

After all, remember, the heart of the matter has been to help women get a feel for the game.

This is a great story of love. A love that makes a man who is thought to be non-emotional, very emotional—moved by teamwork, moved by strategy, moved by execution, moved by scoring, and moved by winning, because of his love for the game.

This great story of love is demonstrated when alumni of high schools come back to give back and support their alma maters year after year because of their love for their high-school football teams.

This great story of love is demonstrated when former high-school football teammates have formed alliances, friendships, and brotherhood for life because of what once was a mutual mission, which has now become simply a mutual love for the game.

This great story of love is demonstrated when alumni from colleges and universities all over the country come back to give back and support their alma maters year after year because of their love for their college football teams.

This great story of love is demonstrated when former college football teammates have formed alliances, friendships, and brotherhood for life because of what once was a mutual mission, which has now become simply a mutual love for the game.

This great story of love is demonstrated when former professional football players, now in the elite fraternity of NFL alumni, maintain those memories of going into battle together on every Sunday or Monday in one of the many NFL stadiums around the league. These former teammates have also formed alliances, friendships, and brotherhood for life because of what once was a mutual mission, which has now become simply a mutual love for the game.

I love this game of American football—this is my portrait.

Remember, whether it's a football team or a relationship team—joint effort and synergy create a winner.

Index

Symbols

3-4 defense, 41
3-and-out, 50–51, 51
3rd down conversions, 35, 36, 50, 89
4-3 defense, 41
8-in-the-box, 46

A

aggressive approach, 53, 82
   example of, 58–59
   vs. conservative approach, 29–30, 44,
      82–83
aggressive attack, 44
alliances
   about, 17, 18
   and the mutual mission, 19
   and the *us against them mentality*, 18
   author's examples of, 17–18, 18
   in the locker room, 66
   role of, in developing team culture, 19
alone on an island, 41
alpha-male, 39, 44
American football team. *See* football
   team.
Andersen, Morten, 108
audibles, 91–92
average yards per carry/rush, 34

B

balanced attack, 29, 32, 34, 48, 86, 106
black zone, 94, 95, 96
blitz, 92
blockers, 56, 57, 59, 80.
   See also special teams: players on.
blocking, 14, 26, 27, 28, 56, 57, 59
Bob-n-Weave, 107

C

celebrations (of scoring), 107–108
   as a team, 107
   Bob-n-Weave (St. Louis Rams), 107
   Fun Bunch (Washington
      Redskins), 107
   Lambeau Leap (Green Bay
      Packers), 107
   Mile High Salute (Denver
      Broncos), 107
   individual celebrations, 107–108
center, 26, 31.
   and snapping, 26
   compared to long snapper, 56
   in formation, 26, 40
   See also offensive linemen; offensive
      team: players on.
change of possession, 93
Chicago Bears, 108–109
circle of communication, 71, 76
coaches
   and alliances, 17, 19
   assistant coaches, 75, 79.
      in huddle, 73
      See also coaches: position coaches.
   coaching styles
      aggressive approach, 29–30, 44, 53,
         58, 82–83
      balanced attack, 29, 32
      conservative approach, 29–30, 44,
         82–83
   defensive coordinator, 20, 79
      and game plan, 91
      in huddle, 73
   featuring star players, 85
   head coach, 20

(defensive team, continued)
  and securing a turnover, 93
  and situational preparation, 43
  and sure tackling, 48
  and takeaways, 93
  and the turnover ratio, 50, 51
  as score stoppers, 39, 51, 103–104
  compared to offensive team, 25, 39, 44
  goals of, 43, 103–104
  lines of defense, 43
  plan of attack, 44
  players on, 39–42
    See also cornerbacks; defensive line-
      men; linebackers; safeties.
    attitude of, 39, 45, 48
  strategy of, 43, 48–49
    8-in-the-box, 46
    aggressive approach vs. conserva-
      tive approach, 44
    aggressive attack, 44
    based on field position, 44
    blitz, 92
    force turnovers, 89
    making opposing offensive team
      one-dimensional, 46–47,
      87–88, 106
    pass coverage, 47
    pass rush, 47, 50
    prevent defense, 89
  success of, 50–52
  types of defense
    3-4 defense, 41
    4-3 defense, 41
    8-in-the-box, 46
    dime defense, 42
    dime package, 42
    goal-line defense, 49
    nickel defense, 42
    nickel package, 42
    pass defense, 44, 49, 49–50
    red zone defense, 50, 51
    run defense, 44, 48
    short yardage defense, 49
defensive team meeting, 19, 20
Denver Broncos, 107
dime defense, 42
dime package, 42
directional punt, 54

distance, 81
  as a factor in play calling, 30, 45, 83, 84
double-team, 58, 80
down, 81
  as a factor in play calling, 30, 45,
    83–84
drop-a-set, 41, 58, 82

E

emotions of the game, 97, 100
end zone, 36, 94, 96
  and scoring a touchdown, 105
  goal line, 94, 96
execution, 91–101
  and communication, 75
  and momentum, 101
  and zones of the football field, 97
  compared to quality time, 91
  preparation for, 79, 83
  sticking to the script, 91
  vs. good on paper, 100
  vs. hype, 101
extra point, 105, 106
  and the kicker, 104
  vs. field goal, 105–106
extra-point team, 86

F

fair catch, 55
featuring a player, 85
field general, 25
field goal, 51, 104, 105, 106
  about, 105
  vs. extra point, 105–106
field-goal team, 62, 86
field position
  about, 84
  and directional punts, 54
  and special teams, 60–61, 84, 104
  and strategy, 37
  and tendencies, 81
  and turnovers, 37, 51
  and zones on the football field, 95
  as a factor in play calling, 30, 44, 45,
    83, 84
  good vs. bad, 30, 84, 92, 104
  importance of, 60, 61, 92

football
  as a game about gaining territory, 86
  as a game of inches, 87
  as an emotional game, 16, 97, 98–100,
      104
    long-face syndrome, 16
    out-of-control emotions, 97, 98, 99
  as a physical game, 16, 34, 39, 43–44,
      48, 53, 111
football field
  50-yard line, 94
  goal line, 94, 96
  length of, 94
  midfield, 94–95
    and field position, 95
  open field, 43
  out of bounds, 87, 88
  zones, 94–97
    black zone, 94, 95, 96
    compared to a relationship, 97–98
    end zone, 36, 94, 96
    and scoring a touchdown, 105
    goal line, 94, 96
    gray zone, 95, 96
    red zone, 36, 50–51, 89, 95, 96
football team, 13–62.
  compared to a relationship, 13, 13–14,
      22–23, 66, 70, 82, 90, 92
    and importance of communica-
      tion, 75, 76
    and mutual mission, 18
    execution: quality time, 91
    regarding the rules of engage-
      ment, 83
  composition of, 14, 23, 90
  definition of, 13
  See also defensive team; offensive team;
      special teams.
formation, 92
fragile confidence, 16, 54
free safety. See safeties: free safety.
fullback, 28
  about, 14
  See also running backs; offensive team:
      players on.
fumble, 36, 50, 60, 62, 95
  and sudden change, 93
  in the black zone, 95

Fun Bunch, 107

G

gaining territory, 36, 43, 55, 81, 86, 93
  moving the sticks, 86
  secure a 1st down, 29, 54, 81, 84, 86,
      105
game clock, 30, 32, 46, 85
  stopping, 87, 88
game plan, 80, 82, 91
  featuring a star player, 85
ghosts of gains, 60
goal line, 94, 96
goal-line defense, 49
good on paper, 100
  vs. execution, 100
gray zone, 95, 96
Great Dane, The, 108
Green Bay Packers, 83, 106–107, 107
guards, 26, 31
  See also offensive linemen; offensive
      team: players on.
gunner, 58
  See also special teams: players on.

H

halfback, 28
  about, 14
  as star player, 14
    being featured in a game plan, 85
  See also running back; offensive team:
      players on.
halftime, 30, 33, 72
halves (in a game), 33, 72
  and timeouts allotted, 87
  and the two-minute warning, 87
hands team, 57–58
hang time, 54
head coach, 20
  and game plan, 75, 79, 85, 91
  and strategy, 79
  and verbal communication, 75
  in huddle, 73, 76
  responsibilities of, 79
headhunter. See gunner.
holder, 54
  about, 56

(holder, continued)
  and the kicker, 56
  and the long snapper, 56
  laces out, 56
  See also special teams: players on.
huddles, 71–76, 92
  and officials, 74
  as a circle of communication, 33, 71, 76
  call for the next play, 71, 76
  in the locker room, 73, 76
  secret communication, 71, 76
"hurry-up" offense, 88
hype, 100
  vs. execution, 100–101

I

incomplete, 34
incomplete pass, 34
  as a way to stop the game clock, 87
Indianapolis Colts, 58, 83
individual goals
  and team goals, 13
infractions, 74
in space, 43
interception, 36, 41, 50, 60
  and sudden change, 93
  and the free safety, 42
  in the black zone, 95
island, alone on, 41
isolation plays, 31, 32, 49, 86–87

J

Jackson, Rickey, 48
Jersey of the Journey, 110

K

key plays, 100
kick coverage, 59, 61, 62
kickers, 57
  about, 53–54
  and extra points, 104
  and field goals, 104
  and scoring, 104
  and the holder, 56

(kickers, continued)
  and the long-face syndrome, 16
  and the use of tees, 53
  See also special teams: players on.
kicking game, 59
kickoff, 57
  as option at coin toss, 72
kickoff return
  as option at coin toss, 72
  if fumbled, 108
kickoff-returner, 56
  vs. coverage men, 57
  See also special teams: players on.
kickoff-return man. *See* kickoff-returner.
kickoff-return team, 62, 104
  hands team, 57–58. *See* hands team.
kickoff team, 62, 104
  on-side kick team, 58
kick returns, 59, 61. *See also* kickoff returns; punt returns.
kick-returns team, 61

L

laces out, 56–57
Lambeau Field, 106, 107
Lambeau Leap, 107
lead by example
  about, 21
left guard. *See* guards; offensive linemen.
left tackle. *See* defensive tackles; offensive tackles.
linebackers, 46, 49
  about, 41
  and alliances, 17
  as run stoppers, 48
  as star player, 15
  Jackson, Rickey, 48
  middle linebacker, 41
    as signal caller, 71, 72
  Mills, Sam, 99
  outside linebackers, 41
  vs. quarterback, 47
  vs. running backs, 41
  See also defensive team: players on.
line of scrimmage, 26, 33, 46, 47, 49, 86
  and signal callers, 71

offensive tackles, 31
  left tackle, 26–27
  right tackle, 26
  See also offensive team: players on.
offensive team, 25–37
  and 3rd down conversions, 35, 50, 89
  and the physical factor, 34, 48
  and red zone success, 36, 37, 90
  and the running game, 33, 48
  and scoring, 25, 37, 103, 106
  and situational preparation, 28
  and time of possession, 36, 37, 90
  and the turnover ratio, 36, 37, 89–90
  as aggressor, 89
  as point producers, 25, 37, 103
  compared to defensive team, 25, 39,
    44
  goals of, 103, 106
  players on, 25–28.
    and injuries, 45
    See also center; offensive tackles;
      quarterback; receivers; running
      backs; tight ends; offensive
      linemen.
  strategy of, 48, 87
    and the "hurry-up" offense, 88
    and the two-minute offense, 88
    balanced attack, 32, 34, 48, 86, 87,
      106
    decision to punt, 54
    long scoring drives, 111
    two-point conversion, 105
  strong side of, 42
  success of, 35–37, 89–90
  types of plays
    isolation plays, 31, 32, 49, 86–87
    power plays, 31, 86
    setup plays, 31, 32, 49, 86
    play action pass, 49
offensive team meeting, 19, 20
one-dimensional
  as goal of the defensive team, 46–47,
    87, 106
  plays, 86
on-side kick team, 58
on the island alone, 41
out of bounds, 87, 88
out-of-control emotions, 97, 98, 99

P

pace, 92
pass coverage, 47, 50
pass defense, 44, 47, 49–50, 50
passing game, 27, 29, 34, 46, 47, 49–50,
  92, 105, 106, 110, 111
passing plays, 27, 28, 34, 39, 40, 41, 42,
  47, 80, 106
pass rush, 47, 50
penalties, 74
personalities, 15–17, 20
  alpha-male, 39, 44
  cocky player, 15
  confidence shortage, 44
  confident player, 15
  fragile confidence, 16, 54
  locker-room bully, 67–68
  locker-room exhibitionist, 69
  locker-room leak, 67
  locker-room legend, 68
  locker-room play-by-play
    announcer, 67
  selfish player, 15, 22
  team player, 22
  tenacious player, 15, 16
  timid player, 15, 16
    manhood minimized, 15–16
personnel, 32, 91
  and tendencies, 81
physical exchange, 26
physical factor, 34, 48
Pittsburgh Steelers, 83
placekicker. *See* kicker.
plan of attack, 80, 82
play action pass, 49
play clock, 33
players
  and alliances, 17
  and transitioning from the game, 100
  preference of coaching styles, 82–83
  sleeping through meetings, 20
  See also defensive team: players on;
    offensive team: players on.
position coaches, 20, 79
  defensive backs coach, 42
  defensive line coach, 40
  in huddle, 73

(receivers, continued)
   vs. cornerbacks, 27, 41
   vs. the free safety, 42
   See also offensive team: players on.
reception, 34
red zone, 36, 50, 89, 95, 96
red zone defense, 50, 51
red zone success, 36, 37, 89
Reggie Jones' Rules, 74
relationship
   bedroom compared to a locker
      room, 65
   compared to a football team, 13,
      13–14, 22–23, 66, 70, 82, 90, 92
      importance of communication, 75,
      76
      mutual mission, 18
      quality time: execution, 91
      regarding the rules of engage-
         ment, 83
   compared to zones on a football
      field, 97
return, 55
rhythm, 92
right guard. *See* guards; offensive
   linemen.
right tackle. *See* defensive tackles;
   offensive tackles.
RJ's Rules, 74
role players
   about, 14
   and scoring, 104
   and the offensive linemen, 26
rules of engagement, 82
   in a relationship, 83
run defense, 44, 47, 48, 80
running backs, 14, 25, 27.
   about, 28, 33
   and alliances, 17
   and the running game, 106
   as a receiver, 28
   as role players, 14, 28
   as star players, 14, 15, 28
   attempts to tackle, 39, 40
   in formation, 28
   position coach of, 28
   vs. cornerback, 41
   vs. defensive ends, 40

(running backs, continued)
   vs. defensive linemen, 39
   vs. defensive tackles, 40
   vs. linebackers, 41
   vs. nose guard, 40
   See also offensive team: players on.
running game, 29, 33, 34, 46, 92, 105,
   106, 110, 111
running plays, 27, 39, 40, 41, 42, 46, 80,
   106
   definition of, 33
run stoppers, 48
   defensive tackles, 40
   the nose guard, 40
rushers, 56, 57
   See also special teams: players on.
rushing plays. *See* running plays.

S

sack, 39–40, 40, 47, 80
   coverage sack, 47
safeties
   about, 42
   and alliances, 17
   free safety, 46
      about, 42
      position coach of, 42
      vs. receivers, 42
   strong safety, 47
      about, 42
      position coach of, 42
   See also defensive team: players on.
safety (score), 94, 105
score
   as a factor in play calling, 31, 46, 83,
      85
      in relation to time, 85
scoreboard, 37, 51, 80, 85, 104, 110, 111,
   112
score stoppers, 39, 51, 103–104
scoring, 103–113
   all-time leading scorer in NFL
      history, 108
   and change of possession, 93
   and creation of uncertainty and antici-
      pation, 104
(scoring, continued)